OFF THE WALL FAVORITES

Paul J. Volkmann

authorHOUSE®

AuthorHouse™
1663 Liberty Drive
Bloomington, IN 47403
www.authorhouse.com
Phone: 1-800-839-8640

First published by AuthorHouse   06/20/2011

ISBN: 978-1-4567-4878-4 (sc)
ISBN: 978-1-4567-4877-7 (dj)
ISBN: 978-1-4567-4876-0 (ebk)

Library of Congress Control Number: 2011902999

Printed in the United States of America

Photo by Keith E. Lewis Photography

Dedicated to my parents, Dr. Ernest W. Volkmann, who was a chemical engineer; and my mother, Beatrice, who had a passion for writing as well, and was my life-long proofreader.

INTRODUCTION

"Off the Wall" columns, featured in The Latrobe Bulletin newspaper, are a collection of many of my antidotes published over the last decade. The intent of these writings has been to bring smiles to the faces of my readers, in addition to stimulating readers to meditate about many aspects of life. Often people have approached me and commented, "You're a goofball," "I really enjoyed your column this week," or "You made me think."

Frequently I have been asked, "How do you come up with a story week after week?" I have but one answer. God continues to bless me and gives me the inspiration I need. It is as simple as that.

Each of the stories you are about to read is arranged categorically according to a number of general themes. Some of these are true, others fictional; some were told to me and a good many resulted from experiences I have had.

You will notice I mention individuals in some of my columns. The names and their hometowns have been changed to protect their identity. The only names I have kept true to form are the nursery rhyme characters: Little Miss Muffet, Dick, Jane, Spot, Ken and Barbie; icons of the past.

As a result of the Internet, readers throughout the world have read my writings. Based on their comments and critiques, I have selected a portion of those articles for this book.

I hope you enjoy reading them as much as I took delight in writing them.

PREFACE

Back in March of 2000, I had an idea. Why not see if I could have a weekly column in the Latrobe Bulletin? After all, numerous letters of mine to the editor had already been published.

So, I contacted the paper's editor, Marie McCandless, about this possibility. I recall her asking, "Just what would you write about?" I wasn't sure, but I mentioned an interest in writing stories about the police department, things happening around town, and thoughts and experiences I have had over the course of my lifetime. She agreed with my proposal. I have been given the privilege of writing "Off the Wall" and "Inside the Outdoors" ever since.

Initially, subscribers of the newspaper were the only recipients of my columns. Now, I can humbly say, people all over the world read my writings and look forward to my commentaries. Even servicemen defending our great country are recipients of emails containing my weekly columns.

I am very thankful to the editorial department of The Latrobe Bulletin and its owner, Gary Siegel, for permitting me to publish my writings, and my loyal readers and friends who have encouraged me throughout this journey. It's been ten years of blessings, and with God's help, I hope I have many more years ahead.

I wish to express my thanks to family members, Mrs. Phillip Westerbeck, who helped edit this book, and Keith E. Lewis Photography.

Contents

On Holidays . . .

NOT FREE

Advertise in the newspaper a thing that is free for the taking, and people will beat down your door to get it. On the other hand, present a way of life to them, and if accepted, it may be a freedom for which they may have to fight. As can be noted, one comes very easily. The other does not.

For centuries now, citizens of our beloved country have been going to battle to uphold the many freedoms we value so highly. These liberties have carried forth in our lifestyles today, and in some cases, even taken for granted.

With that being said, it must be noted that we can't just mention one of our many country's holidays without tying in three of them that really go hand in hand. I'm speaking, of course, of Memorial, Independence and Veterans Days. And, if we didn't have the Fourth of July celebration each year, what would our gallant soldiers be fighting for, if it weren't for those things we treasure so much in the U.S. of A.

Sometime back, as some of you may remember, I walked the streets of Latrobe asking citizens two questions—"Why are you proud to be an American?" or "Why do you hate living in this country?" I really didn't expect answers to the pair, but got replies to both.

Two people told me, "Because of good people like you," and "Because I know you." I quickly laughed that off and moved on.

A lot of citizens said their pride came as a result of relatives serving in the Armed Forces, either in the past or in the present, from grandparents to soldiers in Iraq.

Some statements caught me off guard. A small youngster looked up at me and proclaimed, "Because I live in a house." Unknowing to him, I'm sure, I found that to be very powerful. A woman shared, "Going for a walk." Others said, "Women aren't put down in this country or have to cover their faces." And another—"We can live together no matter color, religion, male or female."

Quite a few people were emotional. One stated, "It is the most moving holiday of the year." One citizen, shedding tears as she spoke, said quietly, "I feel bad for our boys and for everything that is going on in Iraq."

Most all the negative comments centered on our government. "I hate living in this country because the politicians of today are the opposite of those years ago. "They use their office for personal gain." Or, "I don't believe our government has true compassion for the average and below average American." "This country is too money hungry for the mighty buck (the government)," one citizen commented.

One teen told me, "You're making me think." I hope I made more do the same.

There were many who could not tell me any freedoms they valued, or plain refused.

So, was my goal in writing this story to see how many different freedoms people could come up with, or were there more? Anytime I write columns, I do so with purpose. I wanted to create awareness, and also give honor to those who continue to fight the battles, so that we may hand down these freedoms to our children. I was looking for one answer that never was brought up—the right to vote. Only once in an email did one person mention this all too important freedom.

Remember the headlines of the last election—"Light Turnout Expected?" Why do people snub their noses at something so important? This is a right for which our veterans fought. Shouldn't we cherish it as part of our democratic system?

I was also seeking to hear more about education. Here again, one person told me, "We have the right to get a good education." People in so many foreign countries don't have the opportunities we do. We are given the chance to make something out of our lives; but sometimes I feel people do not exceed their comfort zones, and try harder to do their best.

Could it be that the purpose of this column is to bring to light how blessed we are to have so many freedoms? They may seem "free" as we know the word today, but more importantly, we may not be living them, had it not been for our veterans of ages past.

June 28, 2007

CLAUS CRISIS

It occurred to me recently, upon hearing a report on Fox News, that people buying Christmas gifts, and spending for other needs, should do so with cash and not use credit cards. What quickly came to mind was the gang up at the North Pole. Now, I'm not sure how it comes about, how feed is procured for Santa's reindeer, material is purchased for Mrs. and Santa, not to mention how the elves are compensated for their hard work. It really boggles my mind how the jolly fat man and his crew are going to meet expenses this year at a time when the whole world is in an economic crisis.

Then, another thought dawned on me. I wonder if Santa is a member of a non-profit foundation? If one exists, I imagine it might be called S. Claus Foundation, S.C and E (Elves) Foundation or Humanity for Santa. Through such an organization, not only would the gang get necessities at a discount, but they would get it tax-free as well. Also, there are so many other things one has to think about this year in particular. If Claus or his helpers have to fly to a certain someplace to get the threads they need, will there be increased prices? How will that affect the cost of production?

I must make it clear right now, that Santa will be making his trip to each and every home. So, if there are members of the younger generation reading this column, please be advised that he will be coming to your house. If for some reason he doesn't drop down the chimney in the wee hours of the morning, maybe there are grounds for his delay. For example, maybe Rudolph stubbed one of his hoofs, slowing down Santa's ability to race from house to house.

But let's get back to the Claus crisis: We all know that Santa's sleigh doesn't go anywhere unless his animals are pulling it. I often wonder if Dasher eats more than Vixen? Since there are nine reindeer in all, including Rudolph, who rules the roost anyway? Since Rudolph is the leader of the pack, so to speak, is he entitled to a special type of feed over the others? Really does give one something to think about, you know?

That gets me back to our subject at hand, I wonder how much feed is required to nourish these critters on a day-to-day basis? You know, they must be strong all year long. It goes without saying that they have to be kept fit for their one night's travel around the world. Do you suppose Santa has an oblong track that is on his property, and that he instructs Rudolph and his four-legged companions to go around it so many times a day for conditioning purposes? I can't see reindeer being "couch potatoes," so to speak. They have to remain active so that when they are called upon, they have the energy to take to the air and deliver all the presents. After all, they all need that get up and go. This way, you'll never hear Comet saying to Santa, "I'm too tired," "You didn't feed me enough," or "Can't we do this some other night?" These guys have to be ready!

And as to the elves, they also have to be well-fed. Most people don't know that there are as many elves as there are names. Think about their food costs. And what about Mrs. Claus? I hope by now she is receiving her senior citizen stipend.

In conclusion, I believe we must all do our very best to make sure Santa and his helpers get all the support we can give them. Perhaps, in addition to cookies and milk, we can leave a small contribution on the table that will go toward the feeding of the animals, providing clothing for the elves, or a donation toward Santa and Mrs. Claus' Social Security checks. That way, we can be guaranteed that Santa and his team will return next year. Maybe, kids could do their part by sacrificing some toys so that the North Pole residents will have enough food for next year. Just a thought.

December 11, 2008

Harvest Hymn

Last year, after I had my Thanksgiving message published, a gent wrote to me and told me he disagreed with what I had to say. Now, since my thoughts are usually something based on my observations, it is thus an opinionated column as I see the world around me.

In case most of you may not have recalled what I concluded, I drew attention to the fact that T-Day was about eating, "pigging out," as the saying goes, and maybe feeling a little fuller than normal because of all the consumed goodies. The reader said this holiday was about folks getting together, maybe some who haven't seen each other for over a year. This was the time for great family get-togethers.

I like to think both are true. Idealistically, if everyone had the opportunity to do this, everything would be peachy keen. But it doesn't always work out that way. Without going into great explanation, I'm sure it only takes a little bit of imagination to conclude that not only do some people not feast like a king, but maybe they don't have lots, or any, relatives who are able to join them at this time.

So, I asked myself, what comes to mind besides food and fellowship around the dining room table (excluding all-day football on television)? "Hymns" popped into my mind. Often at church we will find a hymn for each season.

One that I am quite familiar with is, "Come, Ye Thankful People Come." The first stanza goes like this: "Come, ye thankful people come, Raise the song of harvest home: All is safely gathered in, Ere the winter storms begin; God, our Maker, doth provide, For our wants to be supplied; Come to God's own temple, come, Raise the song of harvest home."

All four stanzas of this fine hymn speak of the fall season. But there is more to it than that. Too often we sing selections as told to do so, but we never really follow the words or actually hear what we are singing. This song is fabulous, *in my opinion.*

God not only gave us fields to grow our crops, showed us how to nurture them to grow, but provided methods for us to harvest them as well before the winter strikes.

In verse two, we read, "All the world is God's own field, Fruit unto his praise to yield; grant O harvest Lord, that we, Wholesome grain and pure may be." Three—"For the Lord our God shall come, and shall take his harvest home; From his field shall in that day, All offenses purge away; Give his angels charge at last, In the fires the tares do cast, But the fruitful ears to store, In his garner evermore." And finally the last verse—"Even so, Lord, quickly come, To thy final harvest home; Gather thou thy people in, Free from sorrow, free from sin; There, forever purified, In thy presence to abide: Come, with all thine angels come, raise the glorious harvest home."

The lyricist, George J. Elvey, did a superb job of using the analogy of growing, nurturing and harvesting crops and then gathering them in, as is the case when fall comes to a close just before winter begins. Thus, Thanksgiving is celebrated as recognition of divine favor. We gather together to thank Him for our blessings.

But more so, Elvey exquisitely relates that the entire world is God's field, and His crops are His children. The righteous will join the angels; the wicked will be cast into the fire. What he has written is the Master's Word, poetically perfected.

If you have a chance, pick up a hymnal and meditate on these words written to song.

In any case, have a very blessed Thanksgiving with family and friends.

November 15, 2007

Be A Lighthouse

As we round the bend and head into February, many things may come to mind. These may include birthdays, anniversaries, and yes, Valentine's Day.

During this festive occasion, wives or girlfriends may shop for gifts for their hubbies or boyfriends, and men of all ages will visit florists or candy stores to purchase something they know will brighten the lives of those they fondly admire.

I was quickly reminded of one song that could apply on this February 14. It is called, "Love is in the Air."

As I began to hum the tune, for some unknown reason, a lighthouse came to mind. Then the pieces of this puzzle quickly started to come together.

Back on Dec. 21 of last year, I wrote my Christmas message titled, "Out of Darkness." I talked about Jesus Christ as being the light of the world and how people can be drawn to this element via various approaches.

Now, we all know a lighthouse is a tower made out of stone or wood that is wider at the bottom and skinnier at the top, with a beacon that revolves with tremendous illumination 24 hours a day, seven days a week. Most are usually erected on a point of land to guide seamen by night.

Any sailor may say upon seeing such a structure, the blinking light serves as a warning to stay away from the oncoming shore rather than going to it. So, one may interpret the usage of this form of light as being something negative instead of being positive. Don't be so sure.

Light always attracts. It sends a signal. It directs those out in the seas to stay clear of the land that may be too shallow for boats to journey.

But there is so much more to a lighthouse than meets the eye.

Its tremendous light rests on a firm foundation. God's love has been proven to be far stronger than anything man-made.

The beam from lighthouses reaches out to all whom wish to seek its brightness. Christ, the light of the world is always attentive to those whom call upon Him whether it is to praise Him or seek His help. He will never lead us astray or deliver us into darkness.

Knowing that lighthouses exist, comfort pilots of vessels. To those who turn to Christ in time of need know, without a shadow of a doubt, He will give them peace.

One often feels a sigh of relief when such light is spotted. In similar fashion, many turn to Christ knowing that all is not lost, but the aspiration of hope exists.

Tourists always want to take pictures of lighthouses or even paint them.

But when it comes to attractiveness, no one is more majestic than Jesus Christ. Not only is His presence known from port to port, but all over the world.

So, in my opinion, it thus becomes clear that the song to which I made reference earlier in this column now takes on a much more fuller meaning. I now think of that light upon that building as Christ shining His love out to all who receive Him.

We all can be lighthouses. As Christians, aren't we as His disciples told to shine His Light to others? Shouldn't we display His ray of hope as defined in the Holy Scriptures? We all know He loves us. Isn't it His will that we share His love with others?

Yes, just as the song implies, "love is in the air," should we limit it to one day of candy, flowers or gifts of one kind or another, or carry it one step further?

Be a lighthouse. Stand erect and walk according to His Word. Not only will blessings abound from all who are touched, but God will bless those who draw others to His light.

May this Valentine's Day be the beginning of a year full of love.

February 8, 2007

LOVE THIS LAND

In a matter of days, we will once again be celebrating the Fourth of July. To some, it may mean a time for family gatherings, fireworks or the annual parade to which many of us look forward. What popped into my mind were songs I have heard in the past with lyrics talking about the greatness of our country. I began humming them.

The first tune that entered my mind was, "This is My Country." And it is and I love it! I was born here—Pittsburgh to be exact, and am so blessed to be living here among people who love God and share His love in a very beautiful and spiritual way. I enjoy sitting in an easy chair and looking out the window of my home. I can see the Laurel Mountains, an area rich in beauty, full of God's creations, and my playground, where I can roam freely without the worry that harm may come to me. Such is a place where my father and I used to take walks, talk and enjoy the great outdoors.

The song, "America the Beautiful" also says it all, each line meaningful and thought-provoking. "O beautiful for spacious skies, For amber waves of grain, For purple mountain majesties, Above the fruited plain! America, America, God shed His grace on thee, And crown thy good with brotherhood From sea to shining sea." Wow, what a song! All one needs to do is sing the first verse, and stop, and ponder what was just said.

I still lean toward my favorite, it becomes my "inner-soul" song every time I hear it. It's called, "God Bless the USA" and it was written and composed by Lee Greenwood.

Don't just sing the phrases as though they are words to any old song, but draw them in to your inner most being, and let them become a part of you—"If tomorrow all the things were gone, I'd worked for all my life. And I had to start again with just my children and my wife. I'd thank my lucky stars, to be livin' here today. Cause the flag still stands for freedom and they can't take that away. And I'm proud to be an American where at

11

least I know I am free. And I won't forget the men who died, who gave that right to me. And I gladly stand up, next to you and defend her still today. Cause there ain't no doubt I love this land, God bless the USA."

There are a lot of guts to this song—truly, right to the core, and nobody can tell me otherwise. What it tells me is every time we see our flag, it should spell out freedom, liberty and independence to all whom are citizens of our country. And as long as our flag keeps flying, we should not just exercise freedom any old way, but do so responsibly, reflecting our values in a positive light so others may understand who we truly are.

Not just material, that same flag has been passed down through the ages. Men, through many years, have carried it and they still cling to it today. We must not forget to continue to pray for our military fighting for us overseas. They are freedom creators and we should hold them in highest esteem.

So, what are you really thinking in terms of this upcoming celebration? Is the parade your big attraction for the Fourth? Or are the fireworks the real reason you enjoy this holiday?

In the final stanza of his masterpiece, Greenwood spelled out the convictions that we all should hold dear—"And I gladly stand up, next to you and defend her still today. Cause there ain't no doubt I love this land, God bless the USA."

A little post note: My son, Aaron, called while I was writing this column. I told him I was writing a story for the Fourth. He started singing, "America the Beautiful." I then explained that these songs were my subject matter. He called it a "Volkmann thing!"

July 1, 2010

MARY DID YOU KNOW?

In a matter of days, we will be celebrating Easter. For Christians, this is the most festive weekend of the year. People will flock to churches, to not only make their presence known, but to worship their Lord who died on the cross on their behalf.

Forty days previous to this Sunday, many faithful followers have been steadfast, either by foregoing something or giving of themselves as part of the Lenten season.

Before that time period, we were still feeling joys generated by Christmas. I remember a few days after the 25th, I saw on television, groups of people singing Yuletide songs. One of these was called, "Mary Did You Know?" The words raised questions about Mary's newly born son, Jesus Christ.

One stanza went like this: "Did you know that your baby boy is Heaven's perfect Lamb? This sleeping child you are holding is the great I AM." All the stanzas were exquisite. I thought, "I wonder if Mary knew the son she was about to bear was going to be someone out of the ordinary?"

On the other hand, here was a woman who was totally obedient to God, well before Jesus Christ became man. She was not just another woman. God picked her to carry our redeemer because of her devotion to our creator. There is no question in my mind that she was indeed very special in every sense of the word. After the angel told Mary that she, a virgin, would bear a son, Mary fully accepted the fact and continued her reverence to God.

In asking the question, "Mary did you know . . ." would be no different than asking any parents if they knew what professions or lifestyles their children would have in the future years. We have no way of knowing.

If I could change the song a bit, I would first add two or three more groups of words continuing with, "Yes, I believe that Mary knew God's love that Christ would bring. Yes, I believe that Mary knew such joy that we now sing . . ."

Yet, do I believe she knew that her son would die on the cross to free man of his sins? It is my opinion she knew nothing of it, any more than I know how I will die. Regardless, she had devotion to God before Jesus' birth, during His life and afterwards. Her faith in God never wavered. As true Christians, we should follow her example.

I might even write a final stanza that would go something like this: "Sinners do you know upon the cross, our beloved Lord He died? People do you know, below the cross, His mother stood and cried? It was He who took His life, our salvation was His goal. By giving all our live to Him, He will make us whole."

But that's not the end; there will always be more questions. In this case, do you suppose Mary gave any thought to His rising from the dead on the third day? There was nothing written on stone that would tell her the destiny of Her Son.

It happened, didn't it? Believe it or not, it is fact. For centuries we have had a book that is said to be the most read literature in the world that tells this wonderful story. Some people call it the Holy Scriptures, others speak of it as the Holy Bible. In it is the greatest story ever told—Christ's birth, His walk and death for us and His glorious resurrection.

So, as we conclude with Holy Week and give reverence to our Lord, who gave of His life freely on Calvary on the day we celebrate as Good Friday, may we as believing people never forget that God sent His Son into this world to accentuate the fact that His Father is a living, loving person full of mercy and grace.

For it is written in John 11:25, "I am the resurrection and the life; he that believeth in me though he were dead, yet shall he live; 26. And whoever lives and believeth in me shall never die."

May each of you have a very blessed Easter.

March 24, 2005

On People . . .

YUCK!

Often when we visit our son in Aspinwall, just outside of Pittsburgh, he takes us to one of his favorite restaurants where we have a very nice informal get together.

The first, a full service restaurant to which we feasted was in Oakmont. My wife fell in love with the place after trying various entrées and loving each one of them. For a period of time, we always found ourselves going back there.

Now, I have to admit, I liked the choices on the menu as well. I found selections that were unknown to my taste buds. So, not knowing if I would like them or not, I found myself picking food that I hoped I would savor.

While everyone else was choosing everyday preferences, I decided to try the largemouth bass sautéed in yogurt. That wasn't only good, It was simply great!

I also saw that fluke was on the menu. I said to my wife, "The next time we come back here, that will be my pick." But in the meantime, we decided to go elsewhere just for a change of scenery.

Since a Chinese restaurant was nearby my son's apartment, we decided to give that place a go. So, recently I tried eel don, a combination of eel, ginger, seaweed salad and rice. Most excellent, to say the least.

I was talking to a friend lately, telling her about my wonderful get-togethers with my son and that we ate at this restaurant, and I had eel. With that she belched out a guttural, putrid sound and gave me a very horrid expression. I asked, "Have you ever eaten eel before?" with which she replied, "No!"

How can someone comment to the negative about something if he (in this case, she) has never eaten a substance before?

But she wasn't the first person who has exclaimed similar outbursts.

A friend calls me nightly, and we do bring up the subject of food often, particularly around Lent. He has emphatically told me how much he hates eating fish, and makes no bones about letting me know this annually.

Lately I asked him about eating tongue, liver, whale, or brain. He told me he hates them all. I then had to ask about each item individually.

"Have you ever eaten tongue?" I asked. "Yuck!" he shouted back through the telephone's receiver. "That doesn't even sound good."

So, as is my habit of interrogating people, I had to continue. "How can food sound good?" I asked him. His comeback was, "You know what I mean." I guess he didn't like that question. I asked this middle-aged man to explain his comments.

In so many words and more, he suggested that anytime one mentions a body part of an animal that is not on a usual menu such as those cited above, it doesn't sound good to eat at all. So even though he has never tried them, and in all likelihood won't, he concludes that they all must taste pretty horrible.

It's too bad, you know. I was raised on some foods that I thought were exotic. Each year, my father would get a big wooden container of oysters sent to him as a Christmas present from an associate. The whole family delighted in eating them. My mother served us cow's tongue regularly, as well and we all developed a taste for it. One outing to Pittsburgh, the wife and I visited a restaurant where I ordered whale. Tasted just like beef. I was given a whale of a portion to boot!

If given a chance to try a food you've never eaten, go for it. You just may *love* it!

January 24, 2008

WILD WILLIE

Riding with Willie ought not to be a frightful experience, for my middle-aged friend is usually a very careful driver, and seldom disobeys the laws.

But his habits can vary, so I found out one sunny, summer afternoon.

It was a Saturday. As usual, Willie picked me up and we headed to St. Vincent Basilica for an hour of confession. We then would proceed to the mall or a familiar bookstore where we would enjoy each other's company before heading home. There was always a definite time of pick-up and hour of return.

This day was no exception. Ritualistic activities usually occur in some pattern. This was ours.

As the story goes, my friend, in his two-door red coupe, pulled up to my curb, smiled at me through the closed glass window, and I proceeded to get in. We greeted each other pleasantly, he put the car in gear, and we slowly headed toward our destination.

So far, nothing was out of the ordinary. Willie stuck to his slow-to—moderate speed as he traveled through downtown Latrobe in the left lane, all the time chit-chatting with trivialities that seemed to pass the time as we motored closer to the church on the hill.

On the other side of town, we turned left up one of the main avenues, when all of a sudden, the south side resident proclaimed, "Do you remember this band back in the 60's?" Musical vibrations were echoing from speakers located in the middle of the dashboard.

I studied the series of notes and had to admit, nothing sounded familiar.

Then all of a sudden, Willie did the unexpected. He actually bent over and started fiddling with the buttons all the time stating, "Well, if you just hear this next song, I think you'll recognize the band."

Now, I know we're going to confession, but I was hoping he was not arriving there to state that he had just demolished his car and injured his best friend, who could not recognize some short-lived foursome that supposedly made musical history. There's got to be a time and place for everything, and this was surely not the time to nose his way along the keys of the control panel in search of the right button to push.

"Get your head back up and watch what you're doing!" I screamed at my driver.

Abrupt outbursts do help in matters like this. It worked, so I thought.

But Willie was determined to find the song for me. Down went the head again. I couldn't believe what I was witnessing. My conscientious chauffeur was conducting his modusoperandi far off course. I couldn't believe what I was seeing.

"Look out for those mailboxes!" I exclaimed as I sat on the edge of my seat. "Hey, we're heading straight for that row of fencing," I bellowed out.

"I see them, but you have to hear this song. It's really great! It will really help you feel relaxed!" he said in a very calm tone.

I thought to myself, "How can I feel any kind of calmness with fence posts, mail boxes and telephone poles approaching the front of the car?"

Just then, a group of notes filled the air. "I know that one," I proclaimed. "That's by the Five Satins—'In the Still of the Night'! That was definitely a great song."

Then the thought occurred to me. If I had told "Wild Willie" earlier that I recognized the first song, none of these strange goings-on would have ever taken place. I could certainly have saved some panic stricken times.

Oh, the trials and tribulations of life . . .

July 7, 2001

Left Behind

So often, we read about people caught up in catastrophes, others traumatized by loss of loved ones, but seldom do we meet individuals devastated by such perils.

Recently while on a trip to Maryland, I met a gentleman who actually experienced disaster first-hand when Hurricane Katrina hit New Orleans.

Roger Wilkins first told me that his wife and many of his relatives left his neighborhood when storm warnings were issued. But for some reason, he decided to stay. His judgment was based on the theory that this hurricane would be no worse than the others in the past.

On that date of Aug. 31, 2005, the retired executive director of the computer department of the United States Department of Agriculture heard the winds whirl over his house and sat patiently in his home with his dog, Peanut. After it passed, he went outside and started taking pictures of the damages for insurance. He was one of the few who took out a flood policy despite others trying to talk him out of it.

At first, Wilkins thought little of the water that lay on the road in front of his driveway. "Then something peculiar started happening," he stated. "The water started rising above the stacked mailboxes. This was very odd." He then hastened back to his dwelling which was up a grade, ran into the living room and started grabbing as many valuables as possible stacking them as high up as he could. Grabbing his dog, Peanut, he then ran to his truck that was parked on a hillside behind his residence. That would be where the two would spend the night.

The next day, Wilkins left Peanut in the truck and went in search of help. "I had no idea what lay ahead. I could see water and debris gushing down my street. This definitely wasn't rainwater. When I left, I had $40 in my pocket and a small bag of possessions in a plastic bag. The water was up to my knees," he explained.

When he was no more than two blocks from his house, he was now wading through water chest high. Cries of help could be heard from surrounding homes, even gunfire from people trying to attract attention. The government retiree had two things on his mind—seeking help and rescuing his Chihuahua.

It wouldn't be until four days later that Wilkins was given a sandwich. "I was so hungry and felt so blessed to be given this," he said, "I couldn't wait to eat it.

When I went to bite into it, a helicopter flew over and covered it in dust and I couldn't bite into any of it," he said.

Word was out, stay away from the Superdome. If given the opportunity, go by bus to Houston. Hearing that seniors were given preference, Wilkins immediately instructed an older man to stay with him. Able to board a bus, they headed to Texas.

Half way there, the bus stopped for gas. Peanut's master attempted to exit the vehicle telling a police officer his brother lived 20 minutes from there. "Let me make a phone call to him and he can pick me up here," Wilkins said. The officer said, "Get back in that bus or I'll arrest you and throw you in jail!"

Taken aback, Wilkins got back aboard the four-wheeler. "I felt so frustrated," he said. When the cop disappeared, others encouraged him to get off and sneak away and hide. He did so promptly, first ducking behind the buses, and eventually finding a Waffle House. Explaining the situation to the proprietor, he asked if he could be hidden there until the bus departed. "They not only told me I could do so under the counter, but gave me a free meal and even called my brother. I had not eaten for over a week, my body was shaky and I was a nervous wreck. I offered to pay, but they said I could eat all the food for free."

Eventually, Wilkins did go home. He was met by a gentleman who lived across the street and stayed at his property which was located above the flooded area.

Upon seeing the retiree return, the neighbor excitedly said, "I've got bad news and good news. Your house is totaled. But, I did rescue Peanut despite being bitten twice and he is fine." Both dog and rescuer have been best friends ever since.

September 21, 2006

Found Fast Asleep

Jane had just gotten off work. She was notified that it was her turn to pick up the kids at the skating arena and take each home. There were six parents in a five-mile circumference and periodically each was called upon to take part in the car pool.

Being a bit fatigued, the Latrobe resident did her duty and drove each teen home to his designated house in the area. Each person arrived home on time. Then, she decided to take the family to an area restaurant where she could relax, have a bite to eat and share some quality time with her kids.

All went well. They arrived at the undisclosed location, piled out, went inside and waited until a table was ready for them. Then they were led to it and given a menu. After five minutes or so went by, the waitress returned and wrote down the orders. Ten to 15 minutes later, the food arrived.

The party of four quickly manned their utensils and dug in. The plates were polished off in no time at all.

During the whole meal and following its conclusion, everyone had something to say. I can only imagine the conversation must have dwelt around the bumps and bruises of the evening activities. Certainly there were even goals met concerning accomplishments that bore excitement.

One six-year old lad found that the late hours were getting a bit much for him and began dozing off at the table. The combination of late hours and a heavy meal will put many people to sleep. This youth proved to be no exception.

Asking if he could go to the restroom, his mother (who wished not to be identified) granted him permission. Talking amongst themselves, the sharing of thoughts continued for about ten minutes.

All at once, Jane became concerned. Jordan had not returned to the booth. Another member of the family was sent in search of him. No where could he be found.

The manager of the establishment was alerted and his staff stopped what they were doing and everyone looked for Jordan. Someone even suggested going out to the car and seeing if he was there. The vehicle was locked and empty.

Everyone was starting to get a bit panicky. "What could have happened to Jordan?" was the question.

The custodian cleaning the ladies restroom was interrogated. Maybe the youngster wandered in there by mistake. In as much as he could not read which facility was which, there was that possibility. The employee had not seen the youth, he told his boss. The search continued.

Then an idea struck one of the patrons. Before calling the police in on this matter, try to think what would be going through the mind of a six-year old who was very tired and wanted to sleep.

So, the family and the restaurant's staff and manager examined each empty booth to see if the child had curled up on one of the empty seats and gone to sleep. At that time of the evening, not many people were patronizing the premises, so there was a good chance he could be sacked out somewhere in the surroundings. Again, no Jordan.

Finally, one person got a brainstorm and returned to the parking lot. Another question was asked. "Could there be a car that is parked here that looks exactly like the one in which he came?" Several people went from vehicle to vehicle in the dark of night hoping this hunch would pay off.

There he was, fast asleep, laying in the back seat of what he thought was his mother's car. Jane opened the door and called to her son, "Jordan, Jordan, wake up, you are in somebody else's car!" The sigh of relief was heard when the words of relief rang out, "We found him and he is all right!" There are no greater words to a mother than that.

August 25, 2005

That's Funny . . .

The other day, a fellow came into my store. We began discussing the various fish populations in area lakes. Before long, I highlighted some subjects that I thought were somewhat humorous. As he stood there and listened, I could see he was enjoying what he was hearing. Minutes later, he was smiling quite a bit. He then looked down at the floor and proclaimed without as much as a chuckle, "That's funny."

I knew another chap that did the same thing. We would be discussing something and he would not so much as even grin when something amused him. He would look at me very stoically and state the same two words. They came out in the same tone as "He died," "The Butler did it," or "I'm not hungry."

Didn't God give everyone that emotion to laugh out loud? I guess that falls under the category of mysteries of life.

Just the other night, I was watching a program on television called Bananas. It features comedians. Every presentation is jammed-packed full of humorous anecdotes.

The night I watched the tube, a fellow by the name of Mike Williams was sharing his story material. I laughed so loud that tears came to my eyes.

I have been around people who laugh differently than others. Some have a squeak. Others blurt out giggle after giggle after giggle. Persons have been known to snort while releasing bass-type notes. Everyone has heard people laugh aloud to certain degrees. But to be silent and seriously state one's expression? That is kind of odd to me. Yet I have seen it done many times.

I often wonder if the parents of these people told them that they should keep their emotions to themselves and not let their voices be heard. That's a shame, because I don't think that is what God intended when he made us to laugh.

I talked to one senior citizen who was hospitalized recently and she was describing the peril she had experienced. Knowing that she was a bit blue, I decided to see if I could humor her. I related one of my little stories. All at once, she burst out laughing. She thanked me by stating, "Thanks Paul, I really needed that today."

It's been said, "Laughter is the best medicine." I think that tops the chart next to, "An apple a day keeps the doctor away." Sometimes tidbits of humor do help us get over the rough times of life.

One fellow who chauffeurs me to do my food shopping loves humorous stories. To say that he delights in this type of material is an understatement. Since he has a photographic memory, I like to compare him to a sponge. He soaks up all these tidbits and then releases several when in the presence of others.

Make no mistake about it. When this man laughs, one knows there is joy flowing through his veins not to mention from his heart. When he enjoys a joke, for example, he will laugh heartily. When not, he will say, "That is a time joke, I will laugh when I have time."

I asked Sarah Giggel, from Tucson, Arizona, "What are your favorite sounds?" to which she replied, "My kids laughing." I can identify with that. I love to hear kids laugh. As far as that goes, it gives me great pleasure to hear adults do the same.

So, don't hold it in. Let that laughter out. If you have to comment, "That's funny," add a chuckle. It just may do you a world of good and others, too!

July 14, 2005

Bus Folk

Recently, I heard on television that a survey had found that women talk as much as men. Being a man as I am, I begged to differ, not because of my gender, but by way of earlier observations.

A while back, a friend of mine got into somewhat of a discussion concerning my stories. She told me I should not write my article unless I did a great deal of research about the subject at hand. So, instead of letting my fingers do the walking, as many people do, to thumbing through relevant materials in books, etc., a couple of weeks ago, I took a different approach. I put my ears to the test. While taking a bus tour, I decided to direct my right ear toward fellow passengers, one by one, similar to a policeman using a radar gun, and find out who was talking the most.

What I'm about to relate is the whole truth, nothing but the truth, so help me God!

Behind me were three women, two diagonally to my right, and the third directly behind me. To the front on the right were two couples. A little farther ahead to my right was another duo, presumably husband and wife, but then I couldn't be sure about that. They did make a nice pair, though.

Now, the reason I am telling you all this is that the husband and wife said very little to each other on the whole excursion. The two that seemed to be a very nice couple was fun to watch. The wife seemed to always start the conversation; the two would laugh, and then settle down again. This was kind of the rule of thumb with them. I often wondered what would happen if she didn't say anything. Would they be talking at all? That led me to believe that maybe they were just traveling together and having a good time while doing so.

But let me tell you what created the greatest impression on me—those ladies behind me. They were non-stop talkers. If I would have written down each subject they talked about, I would have been able to fill my column in short order. Topics included the play and movie, Hairspray, which by the way, all recommended. It turns out that each was retired; one a nurse, and the other, administrative office secretary to politicians. I also learned the number of grandchildren they each had. One of the trio talked about her experiences on a bus tour to Yellowstone National Park.

"The roads were so windy and narrow, I had to close my eyes and not even look outside of the bus's window," she said. "I was scared to death. I hope I never have to go through that again."

Just then, the announcer on the bus stated that we will be taking a trip on a train that overlooks a river. That same lady, in a quiet tone stated, "Maybe I shouldn't be going on this ride."

Now, I am not one to keep silent, as many of you know. However, I didn't say anything even though I am always interested in how people occupy their lives, even though I don't know them personally.

To my right, as I said before was a couple. I asked the gentleman, "What did you do before you became retired?" Upon questioning, he told me he patrolled the Monongahela River. Many times, he told me, that his wife would accompany him on their yacht. "There were instances," he related, "that I would catch young men trying to stash beer cans on their boats before taking to the waters."

Even though most of the riders on the bus were middle-aged men and women, I noticed two young girls on the trip as well. "Are you two young ladies enjoying the trip?" I asked.

One quickly responded, "I'm not young anymore. I'm even retired." I told her she looked too young to be retired. She told me her age and mentioned she had served in the army and had put in her time. I congratulated and thanked her for her service.

But if there was one person who really captured my attention, it was a senior citizen somewhere in her mid-to-late 80's. Everything she said knocked the socks off of me.

"I love these trips, people and everything life has given me."

It was at this point that I concluded from all my observations that the survey was incorrect. Women don't talk as much as men; they talk more than men!

July 26, 2007

On Faith . . .

To Believe . . .

I can only imagine that some 2,000 years ago, before the appearance of Jesus Christ on this earth, many people were skeptical of the existence of God. Those individuals, not unlike many today, probably felt that because one can't see God, He does not exist.

Remember when our parents told us about Santa Claus and his wife, his workers, and the Easter bunny? We couldn't wait 'til these "real-life" characters deposited gifts under our trees, throughout our living rooms, or hid eggs in places where we had to search for them to place them in our baskets. We were told to believe, have faith and that they then would come through for us. And as little children, we did just that.

But since those days, we have moved on. Many years have elapsed since we looked forward to sitting on the jolly fat man's lap, writing our wants and wishes on page after page, and filling our straw baskets with lots of candy and colored hard-boiled eggs. Those days are past, and so, too, are the beliefs that those characters actually exist.

Oh, but the joy of being a child. There were lots of fantasies, stories and knowledge passed on to us by our parents, grandparents, and friends. We accepted what we were told, because of our beliefs that what our elders said, was pretty much written in stone.

But as a child, we were also taught other beliefs as well.

I remember attending Sunday school once a week before the worship service. There we learned about the love of Jesus. I don't think we as kids really understood what love was. To recall the trio of words "Jesus loves you" was a phrase that I heard repeatedly. We knew He was someone special. It kind of made sense, in a manner of speaking, but not really, because as I mentioned before, I'm not sure a child could truly understand the true meaning of love.

Then when we were introduced to the song, "Jesus Loves Me," things started to really click. Remember the words—"Jesus loves me this I know, cause the Bible tells me so. Little ones to whom belong, I am weak, but He is strong. Yes, Jesus loves me, yes Jesus loves me, yes Jesus loves me, the Bible tells me so."

Now, the few words of that song began to mold the clay that would eventually form the rock on which we believers would stand firm and not allow ourselves to waver.

I never considered myself a weak child, but I was getting the feeling that there was something more than just Jesus being strong. We would grow out of that song, too, growing older, shedding the skins of childhood, and taking on a mature look on life.

As the years mounted, love took on many different meanings, some satisfying inward needs, while others were directed outwardly.

And still, if we look back, did we as adults fully contemplate that simple phrase from that little song—"cause the Bible tells us so"—how much Jesus actually loves us? I wonder.

Connecting the Holy Scriptures to the Trinity, we find it written, "For God so loved the world that He sent His only begotten Son that whoever shall believe in Him might have eternal life." Can we fully contemplate the validity that Our Father had for His creation on earth when He sent His Son, Jesus Christ, to live among those of yesteryear?

It's a matter of fact—Christ did walk the earth. And His love was felt by many. And the skeptics who once doubted God's presence changed their ways and lives.

And could it just be, that these people who have accepted Christ into their lives and learned of His love, also understand that four-letter word as we children did when we were introduced to it in Sunday school? In my opinion, it has been a growing process, little by little, starting from the very beginning. Having matured, we must revert back, and come to God as little children, believing that He and His love are genuine and true in its purest sense. Only then can growth begin spiritually.

May each of you have a very blessed Christmas.

December 23, 2010

HOPE

I was browsing over some books in a discount book store recently when I came upon a book titled, "John 3:16, A Journey to Hope." That opened a whole can of beans for me, because I started to meditate on that scripture verse.

Most everyone can quote it, maybe not perfectly, but to certain degrees, one way or the other.

Correctly quoted, the Holy Scriptures state, "For God so loved the world that He gave His only Son, so that everyone who believes in Him might not perish but might have eternal life."

It's funny, at least to me, how so many people I talk to just can't understand the last two words. Also there is the word "might." That doesn't mean it's a sure thing that all one has to do is declare to some degree that he/she believes that Christ exists to ensure a spot in the heavenly kingdom.

But all in all, that is a quotation of hope, a statement made under the pretense that if one carries through with a committed relationship with our Savior, there may be a chance he will be greeted by St. Peter at the heavenly gates.

If I wanted to dedicate this whole column to talking about hope in connection with the Holy Scriptures, I could quote any number of verses from the Bible. Our whole faith is centered on hope. Without it, we are dead in the world.

I chanced upon a little poem that fit right into this column. Emily Dickinson wrote it, and it goes like this: "Hope is the thing with feathers that perches in the soul. And sings the tune without the words, and never stops at all." I like that. It kind of says everything in a nutshell.

Every move we make, every turn we take, is built on hope.

Lately I've been pondering a lot about Dick, Jane and Spot—don't ask me why. I guess I'm just trying to think how they must have thought in their time and what prompted them to act certain ways.

When Dick or Jane gave commands to Spot, their minds were full of hope that Spot would obey whatever they asked of it, right? The same would apply to our pets—to do something they were trained to do.

My neighbor often tells his dog that it can visit me, but it can't lick me as it wants to do, and it obeys.

Anytime we set out to go someplace in a vehicle, we are hoping to get to our destination. When we have visitors, we hope those coming into our homes will feel comfortable, like the food, and take part in the fellowship.

I haven't talked to a fisherman or hunter who steps into the great outdoors who doesn't hope to bring or drag something home for the dinner table. For the hunter, the word is spelled out in the scope aimed at trophy game to shoot. For the angler, there is hope attached to that hook.

Those who are ill, hope to get well. Throughout the world, prayer chains have been created so that believers in God may pray for others through Christ Jesus. Miracles often result from intercessory prayer. One not only prays to the Blessed Mother or saints living in the heavenly Kingdom, but these requests are directed to Jesus, who in turn pleads with God, that His mercy be granted.

The author was right on target when he said John 3:16 is a journey to hope. But what hope can there be if all one has to do is believe in Jesus Christ, and after one dies he's dead? One has gone off on another path if he thinks that's the guaranteed way to salvation.

But the real glory of eternal life is in knowing that all who have made it to heaven are just as alive as they are here. So when we offer up our prayers to Saints Jude, Theresa or Cecelia, they in turn will intercede for us and God will hear our pleas.

Yes, seek ye first the Kingdom of God, take the journey and then rejoice for that hope in our Creator just may set you free.

September 2, 2010

F.R.O.G.

One day, upon opening up my store, a senior citizen exited his car and noticed my actions as I was positioning a doorstop under my front door.

He yelled, "Pee Vee, you mustn't kick that thing around. That's your dear friend."

What he was making reference to was one of those hard plastic toys that imitate sounds of various types of creatures.

For those who may not be familiar with these "spectacles," manufacturers have produced a number of talking and singing fish, turkeys, ducks, the Caddy Shack Gopher, and a frog that is capable of singing various songs or reciting short sentences when one passes by them. The objects would also "do their thing" if onlookers push buttons which are positioned on their exteriors.

Well, as the story goes, I unlocked my front door around 9:30 a.m. and kicked the frog out from inside my store and slid it underneath my door to be used as a doorstop. After all, it was one of those things I really never wanted anyway. Since the wind often blows my door shut, and selling the frog wasn't in the cards, I decided to put it to good use as a doorstop. Somehow it looked very fitting there.

So, as I kicked the frog into place, my friend, Frank, made a comment about my actions and told me I had to treat "my friend" with gentleness and not to kick him around. I agreed, and never thought anything more about it.

One day, after returning home from my semi-annual trip to the mall, I was in our kitchen, doing a bit of tidying up, when all of a sudden, I started humming "The Rainbow Connection," a song made popular on the television show, "Sesame Street" by one of its characters, Kermit the Frog.

At first, I touched upon a few notes and then stopped. I then started again and continued. I think we all do that. A tune comes to mind, we hum, sing, or whistle some of the melody, and then we either drop it or continue on with it. Sometimes it even remains with us for the entire day.

As I was continuing, I noticed the melody getting louder and louder as I hummed. At that moment, I didn't think that much about my actions, for, like others, I'm sure, I often like to hum my favorite songs.

After finishing putting the dishes away in the dishwasher, etc., I proceeded to the computer to see if any emails had been sent to me. I went through the usual process, scrolled down, and sure enough, the first one appeared. Would you believe it? The subject was titled, "Frog." Now, what were the chances of that happening?

I read over the story, scrolling down a bit more, leading to the bottom line. I was told what each letter stood for: (F) Fully, (R) Rely, (O) On, (G) God.

I then thought back when Frank came to see me that morning. I remembered in particular when he scolded me for sticking the frog under my door in a careless manner.

Then the Holy Spirit spoke to me and reminded me that the world kicks God around a lot, taking His name in vain, disobeying His Word, and gives Him little consideration.

Even though the green, plastic toy was just that, the wisdom of the elderly gentleman left a lasting impression with me. My doorstop had become a symbol, standing for something more than a pond creature. It would remind me that God is always holding the door open for all of us who want a relationship with Him.

In addition, we must always fully rely, respect, and consider His ways over those of the world.

You see, by kicking that frog around, I was reminded I was doing what the unfaithful do best.

I no longer have a price tag on that inanimate object. I think of Frank's advice and how I should conduct my life each day. And to think that I may have never seen the "light" if it hadn't been for the words of this kind, elderly man and the Holy Spirit.

It is proof, that the little things in life are very much a part of a bigger plan.

August 18, 2001

Maybe . . .

Mary Jane Winniger was walking to work. Along her path of travel were beautiful, flowery weeds growing. As her stride increased in speed, it is probable that many things were on her mind—getting to work on time, finishing the spreadsheets and answering the many phone calls that come into the office.

What she didn't take into consideration is, maybe this would be the last time she would be walking the pavement. Due to many reasons, this could be her last day on the job.

Looking back, if Mary Jane would have slowly directed her approach to her place of employment, momentarily slowing down to admire the flowers that God had created for her to enjoy, she would then go on her way. Maybe she could say a little prayer along her way, thanking God for this touch of color that added something positive to her thoughts, rather than comprehending the consumption of her duties that lay before her. She could ask Him to help her through what lays before her in her daily tasks. Now, to my way of thinking, that may be a better approach, wouldn't you say?

Little Billie Sanders was asked what he wanted for Christmas. As he sat on Santa's lap, he thought and thought, and finally exclaimed, "I want a fire truck, a bulldozer, a scooter, fishing rod and another baby boy I can play with so I won't have to play with a sister!"

Santa looked at him in amazement. "I can probably bring you most of those things, but not a new baby brother. You will have to talk to your Mommy and Daddy about that.

When Christmas day came, all the presents that Billie asked for were under the tree for the exception of a new little brother. The four-year old kicked up a fuss. It just may be that this little fellow should be thankful for the many blessings he has received from God, rather than bickering over requests and desires he asked for but didn't get.

When the youngster ripped open the packaging he looked at one item for a few seconds and then moved on to the next package. He never so much as played with his bulldozer or built up the ladders on his fire truck. It was though he took everything for granted that he was automatically going to receive all kinds of gifts and that was that. There was no reason to cherish or give thanks. He expected all that was requested.

There are people who can't afford the wealth of gifts this youth acquired. When they are blessed with one or two items, they treasure what was obtained. It may be that Billie should have a change of attitude and understand that Santa has just so many packages he can deliver in one night's flight, and not all boys and girls can have delivered what he got. Each parcel is a gift from God, and should be cared for accordingly.

And then we have Martin Williger. Married to a very wonderful and loving middle-aged woman, he has fathered five children. They live in a small community of about 9,000. He is a professor at a nearby college and is an extremely intelligent individual.

He and his family love God and attend the local church. They never miss weekly Mass.

Up to the present, Martin has always been healthy. He ate what he wanted, played with and read to his children, and exercised little as he felt he never had time to do so.

One day while at lunch, our philosophy instructor was stricken with a stroke in the lunchroom. He was rushed to the local hospital where he was treated and admitted. After a period of time, he was given a list of requirements by his doctors, including exercising more, eating a healthy diet, and then released. With him he carried a little bag of bottles containing a number of pills that would aid in his recovery.

Just maybe, living a healthier lifestyle may have benefited Martin. A quick walk for at least one-half hour a morning or evening would have possibly prevented his health problems. Eating too much of junk and fattening foods clogging his arteries could have led to his health problems. If Martin wanted to improve his health, his challenges lay ahead. It was up to him to "grab the reins" and head forward.

What then do all three people have in common? What they failed to take into consideration is that God has a plan for each of us. Take time to smell the roses, don't assume that everything you ask for, you will receive, and cherish the body God has given you. These are all gifts. It is up to you to make the best of them.

November 4, 2010

You Did It!

I was riding in a car to an event with a number of individuals sometime back when the subject of stress surfaced. I happened to mention the familiar expression, "I am busier now since I retired than when I was working." Most retirees have agreed with me, that for some reason, they have to say no to requests to do various jobs they never had the chance to even consider when they were working.

I then said something to the effect that I have to watch how much I pile on my day load of activities because I can become stressed to the point of "burning" out. With that the driver of the vehicle exclaimed, "You are bringing stress upon yourself!" Don't we all bring stress upon ourselves to some degree, I ask? Whether having steady employment or being retired, we all have stress in our lives. Some people do well with it, and others don't fare well at all.

I remember when I was in college, and I was asked to write a term paper, I would start immediately, doing my research and digging up anything I could find to ensure that the assignment would be completed in the allotted time. Others waited until the last minute. I could never do that because I would be stressed out of my mind.

While attending my alma mater and also working for the Ashland Times Gazette in Ashland, Ohio, I was given a test, which, by the way, I believe the newspaper assigned to me to see if I was qualified to handle stressful situations.

I was sent to the country club where a golfing competition was taking place. The event started at 2 p.m. I was to photograph 28 foursomes and have an 8x10 photograph to each one of the golfers by 6 p.m. that evening. I got there at 6:30, one-half hour later. Talk about stress big time! But I kept my cool and wasted no time in getting the job done. I couldn't have done it without my trustworthy motorcycle, which I used to travel to the ninth tee off, and then back to the first, to photograph the men. Boy did I feel good after that job.

By the way, I did have some help. Two of the best photographers at the ATG gave me a hand. They taught me everything that I had to know to do my job.

Everyone handles stress differently. Some people have stress levels higher than others. I have come to recognize that mine is on the lower level. But I have also learned to realize when to pull back when pressures build.

The only trio that never exemplified stress in their lives were Dick, Jane and Spot. What a life they had. Can't you just imagine books written with stress-related titles? "Dick Swears at Policeman." "Jane Screams at Her Mom." "Spot Growls and Bites Mailman." "Dick Has Road Rage Problems."

There are so many little things in life that get under one's skin that cause stress to develop. When we feel these little pressures developing, we should immediately do something about them, positively. So often I hear about people who, instead of dealing with these problems, try to conceal them by mentally shutting them out. That approach rarely works. Each person has to go about problem solving in his own way. Personally, I have found that by turning to God and talking over my troubles with Him, my issues are resolved and He gives me peace of mind. That's the great thing about having a committed relationship with Him. We talk, I to Him, and He to me. It's that easy.

Other people may seek out counselors. And the wonderful thing about having a good friend is, he or she *will* be there and *listen* to what one has to say.

The important thing is to calm down and talk *all* problems through. Don't yell, cry or get upset while sharing. That solves nothing. Instead, quietly release one's thoughts.

Take on only the responsibilities that one can handle. Allow yourself some "me time." Taking time off to go to church, confession, meditation is a big plus.

I enjoy fishing. Haven't had time to go. What's that tell you? Do I have to ask?

October 28, 2010

I See It . . .

While growing up, I was never encouraged to wear jewelry, chains holding medals, or the like. A matter of fact, I diverted from that path of parental raising, when just recently I decided to purchase a crucifix that would hang from a chain that I would wear around my neck. Now at the age of 67, I own something I never thought I'd buy. So, one may say, what persuaded me to make the investment? Good question.

To me, it is a sign to others that I stand behind the teachings of the Church I have come to love, Roman Catholicism. Second, I feel closer to my community of believers when I wear it. But third, and maybe most important, when I bend over and see it just below my nose, so to speak, I'm prompted to correct my posture and reform my attitudes so that they reflect those of Jesus Christ and His teachings.

Like so many others, I will admit, I seem to err at times. Possibly, if the cross dangled from my forehead, would I be reminded more consistently of His reflections? I have no doubt that I would. But, since it is out of sight most of the time, I tend to stray.

So many times, I see people wearing religious jewelry and I have boldly asked them why they were wearing the crosses. Each has flippantly told me it was just something that looked nice so they put it on. No one has yet to tell me of a faith relationship to a denomination of the Christian Church. I find that interesting.

Jewelry as a whole is worn for two reasons, I believe—to make the wearer feel good about himself, and to attract others to the person adorned in necklaces, bracelets or piercings, Lord forbid. I say that, because I think it makes people who put metal objects in their eyebrows, belly buttons or tongues look weird.

Not long ago, I was participating in a church event and noticed a gentleman wearing a crucifix on his sweater that must have measured five to six inches in length. If one feels comfortable wearing one such as it, I guess that is his business. But, my smaller piece of jewelry relates the same message—that I am a Bible believing Roman Catholic.

Flashy, outlandish decorations, I can do without. Coinciding with that statement are piercings that display metal objects sticking in eyebrows, belly buttons or tongues, Lord forbid. There are better ways to attract one's attention, in my opinion, than to waste money being stuck with all this stuff which makes people look weird.

I have often wondered why people wear crucifixes under one's clothing. Do they like the feeling of metal dancing across their chest? Maybe they feel closer to God if the metal cross is nearer to their heart. Or, is it that one is waiting for another to pop the big question—"I'll show you mine if you show me yours!"

How many times have we seen women exhibit valentine pendants around their necks? To me, that is a sign that possibly a boyfriend or husband exists and has given their soul mate something signifying their love for the beholder.

In all seriousness, we, who wear crosses, or in the case of Catholics, crucifixes, have an obligation, and this is to wear our medals responsibly.

Just like the pendant person, we should display this particular jewelry with full reverence and awareness that Christ has a genuine love for each one of us, just as that person who gave his sweetheart that pendant.

In as much as that pendant is worn by many, so are the crucifixes. But ask any woman about the heart, and most likely she will light up and talk favorably about her loved one.

Do cross wearers do the same—light up and speak admirably about their Savior?

Sure gives someone something to think about.

As I said before, when I bend down and that crucifix sways to and fro in my midst, I slow down and think what it stands for. Then I realize each time, I better get my act together if I am to live up to His expectations.

And to think a cross-shaped medal on a chain could be so powerful. Wonder if everyone felt that way?

November 26, 2010

On the Unanticipated . . .

In My Car!!!

We had just left our favorite eating hang-out following church one afternoon when my wife asked if I would like to accompany her to the drug store nearby. I declined, as I was not interested in walking the aisles, brushing up against strangers, and smelling medicines after finishing such a fine lunch at our family gathering.

"Here," she said. "Take the keys. You can sit in the car while I do a bit of shopping."

Grasping them in the palm of my hand, I strolled across the roadway dividing the parking area and the various shops and made my way toward the car. Since it was a sunny, blue-skied day, I sensed warmth about my body and was most comfortable, to say the least.

When I reached the vehicle, I selected a key, inserted it in the keyhole and turned. I heard a click, and the lock knob popped up. I then grasped the doorknob, flung open the door, placed my posterior on the seat, swung in my feet, and closed the door.

Thankful it was Sunday, I enjoyed just sitting. I was shielded from the wind, what little there was of it. The interior of the car was warm. I was in perfect peace.

Looking out the window, I could see the bank straight ahead. I started to wonder if that place was still in business, for I never saw anyone patronizing it for some time.

I saw one plane fly over toward the airport. I've always liked watching aircraft go about its travels. Even if there is a helicopter flying above my house, I have to stop and watch the thing go by. My father was the same way. Maybe his enjoyment rubbed off on me.

As I sat in the comforts of my confinement, I began to wonder what my wife was doing in that store so long. But then, I didn't care. It was Sunday. I didn't have to work. Everything was going on around me. I felt time had no meaning. I suppose, if I had a newspaper or even a book to read, I would have felt equally content. But, for some reason, at this moment, I was just happy sitting, looking out of the window, and that was that, or so I thought.

After a half-hour or so went by, I happened to catch a glimpse of an irate person coming toward our car. As she was getting closer and closer, I could tell her gander was up, and I was mystified, to say the least, what the trouble was. After all, in my mind, I hadn't done anything. I was calmly sitting in my car taking in the sights, not bothering anybody, or anyone annoying me.

My uneasiness intensified as she got closer. This was one upset middle-aged woman! For some reason I must have done something to her and I sure didn't know what it was. Finally, she walked up to the car, stuck her key in the keyhole, turned the metal device, opened the door and shouted, "What are you doing in my car? How did you get in?"

I responded somewhat flabbergasted, "What do you mean, 'Your car'?"

She then raised her voice again proclaiming, "You can tell this is my car. I have a "Jesus" license plate on the front," she exclaimed in a loud voice.

"So do I!" I declared. Then she clobbered me with the original statement, "You're sitting in my car!"

Looking all around, I could see no difference between the car my wife drives and hers. I then quietly spelled out the facts that the car sitting beside hers couldn't be ours because it had a purse in the back seat I've never seen before. As it so happened, our daughter had bought this purse but never showed it to me, so I thought that the vehicle wasn't ours.

I apologized and made a quick exit.

There is a bit of irony to the story. This irate resident of Latrobe was no stranger. I have been acquainted with her an on-and-off basis for more than twenty years. A matter of fact, I even employed her son for some odd jobs many years ago. Here is the kicker: We even attended the same church at one time!

But really, what are the chances our key would fit in her car? I guess only so many keys can be made for one lock of the same kind of car. It just so happened that two drivers parked their navy-blue vehicles side-by-side with Jesus license plates on them, in the same parking lot, on the same sunny day, in a small-populated area.

Now tell me, what are the chances?

February 17, 2001

Basket Baffler

Many of us who are long-time television buffs are all too familiar with programming that features videos of people doing what some consider to be humorous activities. Viewers will sit back in easy chairs watching the dilemmas people get into, and in most cases, get a chuckle from their misfortunes.

Such was the case recently while I was shopping at a deli not far from my residence.

It seems a lady had made her way to the deli case, put her shopping basket on the floor, and proceeded to tell the girl behind the glassed-in coolers what she wished to have.

While there, a neighbor happening to see her standing there, decided to pull a prank on her. He snuck up behind her ever so quietly, removed her blue container and hid it in one of the aisles.

When all the food from the deli was wrapped by one of the employees, it was given to the unsuspecting customer. The shopper turned around to put the items in it and was shocked to see that her basket was nowhere to be found.

Can you imagine the expression on her face?

A bit awestruck, she looked all around the floor, behind a column that was nearby, in areas she thought she might have left it, and finally stared down at the floor, and then at the employee behind the counter.

"My basket is gone," she muttered in a soft tone with a puzzled expression on her face.

The sympathetic employee, who also had a doleful look, responded, "Do you think that maybe someone else might have taken your stuff?"

Just then, the neighbor decided that it was time to reappear, and went over and stood next to the baffled female, looking straight ahead, clasping her basket in his hand.

Still, she was so taken by the incident, she didn't even recognize the gent or even bother to see what he was holding.

Finally, the young lady behind the counter put forth the question: "Do you suppose someone else could have walked off with your food?" So, the search was on.

She followed one chap and peered in his basket, and then back to her original starting point where she decided to dig into a blue basket being held by a gent who was standing tall, "oblivious" to the whole situation.

The frustrated, middle-aged resident decided to dig through the man's basket.

"This is my food," she proclaimed in a loud voice. She then peered up into the fellow's face, recognized him, and exclaimed, "John!"

Laughter followed. For some of the onlookers, it was hard to keep a straight face.

By the time I went to check out my food, the young lady had paid for her goods and left the store. But apparently she must have forgotten something and decided to return and get it.

As I was paying for my products, she dashed in behind me, looked me square in the face, and stated emphatically, "You better not take my food either!"

September 2, 2000

YOUR UMBRELLA?

Those who are familiar with William Shakespeare's monologue, "As You Like it," may recall the opening phrase, "All the World is a stage."

I agree.

So many of my stories result from experiences I encounter as if they were performed as a one-act play put into action before my very eyes.

Such was the case of a recent encounter I had, which is best characterized as a case of perfect timing.

Upon entering church and kneeling at the pew, I began to thank God for His many blessings and asked for special graces for those who were ill or in need of prayer.

As I knelt there contemplating on God's goodness, I started to hear raindrops hitting the pavement outside the doors of the church. Unfortunately, my attention was diverted from prayer to the realization that I had strolled to my place of worship leaving my umbrella at home.

This unexpected occurrence entered my mind as a negative kind of advertising, for "the Umbrella Fella," as I have sometimes been called, should always carry his product with him when inclement weather is in the making.

Maybe upon departing from home, I was just thinking about attending church and unloading my burdens unto the Lord, or in a bit of a daze since I didn't get home from my fishing trip until three earlier that morning.

Anyway, the priest proceeded to give a tremendous homily. Both ears were tuned in on what he was saying. All the same, rain was starting to hammer the stained glass windows and at the same time other thoughts were slowly taking over my mind.

Then it hit me. Where is my faith? I've been in situations like this before. God has always taken care of me. About what is there to worry?

After Mass was over, I greeted some fellow parishioners and chatted a bit, nodded to a few others, and made my way to the back of the church (which is really the front of the building).

Here's where the story gets good.

I wanted to take a few minutes and compliment the priest on his message when I found myself in the midst of confusion. When I got back to the area where he was standing, I noticed him taking a trio of people upstairs to view the organ.

Just then, I received word of an unfortunate incident that had just taken place.

It seems that a certain male in attendance, noticing the downpour, decided to lift someone else's umbrella and make claim that it was his. I guess he didn't want to get wet upon exiting the church.

He tried to conceal the black-colored umbrella with a brown wooden handle behind his body and head out the door. Unbeknownst to the culprit, the owner quickly picked up on the incident and pursued the individual, stopping him in an effort to retrieve his possession.

After a slight rebuttal, the merchandise was reclaimed. The fact that there was a crack in the handle was proof that the owner proved his claim.

But here is where the story really gets good!

As we all know, stealing is always forbidden. God made that clear, and so does the law.

But to take something that belongs to a state trooper has to go down in history as a sinful act of the first-degree!

October 21, 2000

Not My Horse!

A while back, while reading *The Latrobe Bulletin*, I happened to chance upon a couple of paragraphs that talked about horses. In it, the author stated that "This animal remembers everything you tell it."

Now, I can't say I've often come face to face with many of these four-legged beauties. However, throughout the years, I had several encounters with them, most with positive outcomes.

I remember one time one of my employees took me to a stable in Greensburg where her Arabian was being kept. She warned me ahead of time to be cautious, because horses can always tell whether you feel them a threat or not.

So, I decided to set my mind in gear and give off an air of love in my heart, hoping the senses of this stallion would pick up on my vibes and we would get along famously.

Shortly thereafter, I was led into a large ring where supposedly she and others could ride their animals or do what they do in this sheltered oval space. Bonnie walked up to her horse and began talking to it. I can only assume she was preparing it for my arrival.

If the article was right, the animal was taking in everything she was saying and would greet me with similar affection I planned to give it. Well, her little talk worked, because we hit it off right from the very start. It was like love at first sight. She even told me her pet usually doesn't take to strange people as easily as I did to it. That must be my inborn pizzazz with the animal kingdom!

Often during vacations to Cook Forest, we would yearly book horseback trail rides with a guide leading. As long as there was a group, everything went very smoothly. If there was one way to describe them, I could pretty much describe them as being robotic.

In a sense, I felt sorry for the horses, for they did the same thing over and over again. I could see in their expressions, they sure weren't happy campers, at least not like we were.

But if there was ever a time that proved that horses do not always comprehend everything we humans say, it was back in 1959 while I was attending a private boys' school in Potter County.

There were three of us who were put in charge of the horses and barn work. Part of our chores included daily grooming, feeding, watering and the wonderful task of cleaning up after these "beasts."

The two fellows who worked along side of me were experienced riders. They could jump on one of the two animals and ride them bare back. I was more of a saddle creature. Of course, riding bare back was out. On a saddle—strapping me down on it would have been better, but, I had to settle for just riding on it hoping that the horse would follow my commands. Sounds easy enough, doesn't it? Since I was a bit new at this, Mr. Experienced, or Tony, rode his horse behind me. I led. We headed off toward the far woods. Our plan was to make a wide circle bringing us back to the barn. Sounded like a plan.

Half way along our journey, which was going swell, by the way, my horse decided to take off into a speedy gallop back toward the barn. I had no choice but to hold on for dear life. Here comes the good part. All of a sudden the saddle slipped and I was riding upside down, underneath the horse, looking up at its bobbing head. No matter what I said to this beloved breed, it would not heed to my commands. Who says a horse listens to everything one tells it? Not my horse!

Now, you kind of have to put yourself in the position I was facing. Imagine riding underneath this animal, your head no more than a foot from the ground, which, incidentally is moving past your face at an incredibly fast speed. To the right are numerous trees with trunks of various widths inches from the horse's side. Should I have ridden it out, cursing obscenities, at this creature that didn't understand clear commands, waiting until we got back to home base for a break in the action?

Thinking quickly, I decided to "hang in there" until I saw a patch of clearing where there weren't any type of growths coming out of the ground. I then pushed off from my leather seat, landing on the leafy soil, thankful I wasn't hurt.

I guess horses, as people, may understand you, but don't always do as you wish.

May 24, 2007

CAUGHT OFF GUARD

Recently, I was watching a television show, trying to relax after a hard day's work as I typically do. I usually do so to try to unwind. With newspaper in hand and dog on my lap, I try to catch up on the happenings around our fair city, as well as to listen to the vibrations of the tube.

It so happened that I was watching one of those legal shows involving clients and attorneys. After a troubled person had made his case to the professional in so many words and more, the lawyer looked at the person and calmly commented, "Swell."

Somehow that tickled my funny bone. That was not the comeback I anticipated at all. A matter of fact, that was the last thing I expected him to say.

I began to laugh a bit more. I was venting my emotions after my toilsome day. As it so happened, I ended up with a full outburst. Even my dog looked at me so as to say, "What was so funny about that?" All I could tell him if he could understand human language—as is the case with most pet owners, I assume he understands everything I say—was that the statement caught me off guard.

It turns out that one of the reasons I watch this program is to garner those unexpected tidbits of humor that I really need as a way of putting the finishing touches on the end of my day. These are the moments that help me relax before I head to my attic chambers for a good night's sleep.

I wouldn't put it past this character to use other such expressions that would put me in the same state of mind.

Have you ever approached a person with a problem, and feel as though you are at wit's end with every positive avenue tried, and are unable to find a solution? You approach someone you consider your best friend thinking you are going to get some real sympathy and a shoulder to cry on. When you meet him or her, you spill the beans, as the saying goes, and the individual's comeback is, "Peachy."

55

That's really not the response you wanted. A matter of fact, such a remark made only adds to the problem. Do people realize that? You might as well use the attorney's comment—"swell." Usually the suffering person needs comforting words and actions, and not adjectives that actually cause more pain.

I've heard people say upon hearing people's troubles, "So what . . ." or "Don't tell me your troubles . . ." or "You are always complaining . . ."

Friends are people to whom we can turn who are always there to listen to our hardships. Sometimes all people need is a sympathetic ear or sounding board to hear their problems. They may even find that while talking about their issues, they end up better understanding their dilemmas and have an easier time going forth to work on solutions.

But for listeners to state, "Peachy, Swell, So what," etc., the get-together turns out to be a hurting experience rather than a helping one.

I remember one person telling me that she married her husband because he was not only her best friend but a soul mate as well. "We can talk about anything and we'll help each other out when problems arise." I like to hear couples speak favorably of their union in that fashion.

About a month or two ago, I met a man who told me that he was married. He stated that his wife was his partner, but not his soul mate. I'm sure many can relate to his declaration. That is why it is important to have best friends, people who will listen, guide and love. Giving of oneself is a wonderful way we can help others help themselves.

There is one gent in Latrobe who I have always considered to be my best friend. He told me that any time I need something to call him and he will be there for me. That is reassuring, to say the least.

Real friends will take time to listen when you need to talk, keep subject matters confidential and help you step by step if need be. They may even tell you truths you may not want to hear. But there is one thing for certain. They won't blurt out, "Swell."

February 23, 2006

Don't See Them

The other day I was browsing over the endless selections of cereals at the grocery store when I spotted a box featuring flakes with blueberries on them.

Now you probably do not know this, but I love those little round balls of goodness.

I recall many years ago, working up at a hotel in Maine. The cook used to send a bunch of us up to the top of roadway to pick blueberries in an area where there were hundreds of these plants to be found. I think I ate more than I picked. When we finished, we would combine our take into one larger container and head back to the kitchen where the she would make the most delicious blueberry muffins as a result of our efforts.

Anyway, getting back to my shopping excursion, I reached up onto the top shelf in the cereal aisle and grabbed onto the product and drew it close enough to me so I could read the label describing the fat, cholesterol and sugar content in a serving. I also had to verify whether the product had whole grain ingredients. If the commodity didn't meet my specifications, I wouldn't buy it.

Everything passed the test. But for me, the real attraction of the product was its blueberry content.

When I got the cereal out of the cupboard the next morning, I opened the box, dumped the contents into the bowl. Guess what? No blueberries. Bah humbug. I thought the cereal's taste was fair, but felt the product could have been a lot better had it contained its advertised fruit.

So, just for the heck of it, I went back to the market and bought the same brand of cereal, this time selecting the box with red raspberries on the front of the box. To make a long but stressful story short, no raspberries were located.

I called the company that produces this product. I told them they were marketing their products in a fraudulent way. A representative apologized.

He said he would send me a coupon to obtain another box of their fine cereal. I told him I didn't want their cereal if it didn't contain the fruit which was shown on the front of the box. He said they'd send it to me anyway.

This is not the only example of things that are supposed to be, but aren't. For instance, have you ever traveled along some of the streets in Latrobe and seen signs with children on seesaws? Do you realize that there are none to be found in our city? Yet, the big signs indicate otherwise.

I remember when my children were young, we would visit my parents when they lived in Latrobe. My father would accompany us to a small playground that was not far from his house that had a seesaw. One of us would steady one of the kids on the wooden plank while another person would apply weight enabling the board to go up and down.

Of all the playground equipment, we had the most fun on that apparatus.

Even when I was a child, I recall the playgrounds I frequented. Each typically had a swing, sliding board and a seesaw. Now these playgrounds provide more diversity with winding sliding boards, towers to climb, monkey bars and a number of other options. But guess what—no seesaws.

I asked one individual the other day if she knew why today's playgrounds don't have these "gravitational toys." Her reply was, "They've been gone now for a good number of years. They are supposed to be dangerous."

My response to that was, "Anything used improperly or carelessly can be dangerous."

Let's take a swing, for example. Start the back and forth movement until a certain height is reached. Then hold on with only one hand. One's balance might shift as a result, causing the swing's motion to change and increasing the chances of being thrown off the seat.

What would happen if a person went down the sliding board backwards or on his stomach? I've seen this done. Wouldn't that be classified under the word, "dangerous?" Think of the bodily injuries one could incur from these actions.

When it comes right down to it, I guess I can understand the removal of the seesaw to a certain degree. But my question still remains, "What happened to my blueberries?"

April 21, 2005

Hi Mary Ann!

Departing from my residence doorway one summer day last year, I stood on the landing to turn toward my steps when I looked upward to the sky and saw a helicopter coming in my direction. As I started down my stairs, I watched intensely, for then I realized this flying machine was on a mission—to not only check me out, but also to follow me wherever I went. Talk about big brother watching, he was up there looking down.

I, too, was on a mission—to get to the doctor's by 2:45 p.m.

As I walked along the sidewalk, I glanced upward and observed this chopper slowly following me. Now, that I found strange. The first thought that went through my mind was, to telephone to the Latrobe Police Department and have Sgt. Bumar pick me up. I didn't know what I had done, but they had found me.

Continuing toward 911 Ligonier Street, I gazed toward the overcast sky. There it was, still following me block by block. Then it hit me big time. "Wow," I thought, "after all this time . . ." I couldn't contain myself. All the pieces fit. I bet that's Mary Ann up there. She is an EMT for one of the emergency medical helicopter companies. I haven't seen her for years! So I raised my arm and started yelling, "Hi Mary Ann! Hi Mary Ann!" It was many years ago when I met her. She taught CPR for the American Red Cross. I had also sung with her mother in the Holy Family Church choir.

As the chopper followed me down to the two-story office complex, I looked up one more time and smiled. I then entered the premises and walked along the carpet entrance until I reached the elevator. Getting in it, I pushed the button for the second floor and up I went. After getting there, I walked to the doctor's waiting room, and headed straight for the sliding glass window where the receptionist sat waiting. I pushed it open and announced, "You can call the airport, now. I made it here safely." I then related the story.

Returning home, I searched the skies, but no helicopter.

The next evening, I decided to walk to Legion Keener Park. With my oxygen tank strapped to my back, I figured all would go well and I would be able to get there and back without any trouble. I was right about one thing. I was able to make it downward and did get to the asphalt pathway. My goal was to make it to the trestle.

Then all of sudden, two unexpected things happened. First, the helicopter showed up and hovered above me in a stationery position. But worse, I had run out of oxygen.

I raised my hands and yelled, "Hey Mary Ann, if that's you, could you help me out?" Nothing happened. I then turned around and began to stagger toward Ligonier St. The chopper stayed right with me. I thought—that's special. I looked up in dismay. I even raised my arms. Nothing. Then I pushed onward until I got to the High Rises. There I stopped and so did the "mechanical bird." Two things again crossed my mind. "Don't think Mary Ann's aboard this flight. She wouldn't leave me like this." Second, "I'm sure the pilot has a radio. Why doesn't he call the police?"

I did work my way up to Ligonier St., turned right, and staggered my way up the hill. The chopper stayed right with me. No, the police did not show up. If they would have been notified by ye "honorable" pilot, I am certain one of our finest would have been there to assist me.

No sooner did I get further up the street then did my "spying machine" make a sharp left and take off. "Hey man," I said to myself. "This is not the time to leave me." But, that he did.

But as serious as you may think this ordeal was for me, I laughed out loud about what had occurred to me this special day. I mean, what else could I do? Any other behavior would have required more oxygen and energy. I've learned so much from that evening's outing. Now, I carry a cell phone. I know my walking limits. And never expect old friends will be in the helicopters that hover above you. Fat chance. On the other hand, you never know where they just may pop up, or in this case, come down to greet you!

June 17, 2010

On Words . . .

ARE WE TO FEAR?

As many of you know who get my emails, I often start out each morning with a "Thought for Today." It gives people something to think about as they go about their day.

One day, I was about to send off a "thought" when all at once it occurred to me that there was one word that troubled me. It was "fear."

The statement I was going to make for a Tuesday, "Perfect love casts out fear," was sound because of its biblical origin. But one of the words from that passage stopped me in my tracks, as the saying goes, and I decided to research the matter a bit more before passing it along.

So, I wrote to those in my address book and posed the question, "If perfect love casts out fear as the Holy Scriptures tell us, then why are we to fear God?"

Almost immediately, I got responses telling me "I DON'T" or "I respect Him."

But, I got others as well.

A learned individual passed on the facts that "Even though there are dozens of words in Greek and Hebrew that have been translated into variations of our word, 'fear' in both of these cases come from the same root that gives us our word 'phobia.' Many words have a number of different meanings, but that isn't the case here. This is about being afraid. One group is being told they don't need to be afraid, that they'd better be afraid."

He then made reference to two scripture verses that have these concepts: 1 John 4:18—"There is no fear in love. But perfect love drives out fear, because fear has to do with punishment. The one who fears is not made perfect in love."

The second reads from Revelation chapter 14, verse 7: He said in a loud voice, "Fear God and give Him glory, because the hour His judgment has come. Worship Him who made the heavens, the earth, the sea and the springs of water."

One man came back with a statement, "Maybe perfect love does not cast out all fears."

One high school graduate explained, "Fear in God's dictionary doesn't mean 'scared of.' Fear in God's meaning is to respect and realize the power of God. It is surrender to His greatness. It's saying, God is so big and I'm not."

Another wrote, "In the verse of that speaks of fearing God, the definition does not have to do with a literal 'fear' (as in afraid), but rather addresses the fact that we are to 'reverence' God. To fear Him is to be in awe of Him loving Him with all your heart."

A student from St. Vincent College wrote, "True fear of God is the beginning of wisdom. Without the grace of true knowledge we cannot know who we love, (which we can run the risk of loving a concept of a 'god' without loving the true God because of our pride) which is born initially from (holy) fear of God until fear is gradually replaced by love. But, a fear is constant, though it changes, I think, as we begin to 'fear' not so much God, but offending Him by sin, usually as we depart from humility."

One young lady theorized, "We're to fear Him until we are able to love Him perfectly—which is probably after death."

I love the answer of one man who wrote me. He summed it up this way: "It says 'perfect' love casts out fear. But who has 'perfect' love this side of heaven? Since we are not perfect, we will have a perfect love of God, and rightly so. He is our law giver and judge and will determine our eternal destiny. The Scriptures also say that the fear of God is the beginning of wisdom. Fear of the divine judgment moves us to contrition for our sins, and this is healthy. But we should strive for attrition, which is fear of committing sin and losing heaven for love of God. Both fear and love of God are graces from God, so we should be grateful for both, while trying to be 'perfect' as our Heavenly Father is perfect."'

Through the help of others, I have been given insight and wisdom concerning my question. My thanks go out to all who helped shed some light to a fuller understanding.

September 8, 2005

EVER SO PRETTY

I was visiting a friend's house recently when I happened to hear an occupant of the residence calling for his pet. Most names of animals are often a bit out of the ordinary, if you ask me. This was no exception.

"Here Pretty Pretty . . . here Pretty Pretty," the fellow spoke aloud calling his feline. I started to wonder what would ever possess anyone to call his pet a double name. If this animal (sorry, cat lovers . . .) is pretty, why not just call it that?

When I grew up "Spot" was a character from a well-known book, "Dick & Jane." The words in the story were "See Spot run." Would either of the two ever think of calling their dog Spot Spot? Don't think so . . .

Maybe it all has to do with the use of adjectives versus nouns. Could it be that by saying an adjective twice, it makes it double the value?

In my teen years back in the 50's, one of my favorite songs was called "Daddy Cool." If we were part of the gang, doing what Daddy recommended, we classified ourselves as being pretty cool. We were definitely doing what it took to be classy and not square. It had nothing to do with being pleasing or attractive as the word may imply, but the connotation was that we were a group that was full of pizzazz.

But our society has taken the word "pretty" and applied it to other usages. To a foreigner, that may be very confusing.

We speak of the weather as being pretty cool/warm or pretty cold/hot. But a nice looking young lady is also considered pretty hot.

Taking into the consideration that pretty means "pleasing or attractive," then it is easy to understand how someone or something could be pretty neat. But when someone is pretty bad, how can that be attractive? Making a pretty bad remark actually demeans something or someone rather than doing just the opposite, right?

"Did you hear about that accident last night? It was pretty awful?" How can something be pretty in one respect and awful in another? Sorry, but it doesn't go hand in hand.

How about "ugly?" "Boy, it is a pretty ugly animal!" Either it is pretty or ugly. I'm sorry, it can't be both.

I knew someone who I thought was pretty amazing. I thought she was gifted, attractive and great to be with concerning sharing common interests.

In the course of my life, I have also known some pretty stupid people. The description fits them to a tee. On the other hand, I have known some not-so-attractive individuals who have also made some poor decisions in life.

Some people who come into my studio and have their photos taken for passports are pretty vain. They insist on my taking the photos more than once at my expense because they tell me I have done a lousy job portraying them in the identification snapshot.

Incidents described as pretty bizarre might be attractive for the Sherlock Holmes types. These patterns of behavior might be issues that attract the skilled detectives, but certainly would not interest most of us.

Along the same line of thinking would be those who are intrigued by pretty gruesome details.

Then there are those who get some kind of high by being pretty vulgar. They think it is great to be that way. I think it's sickening and offensive. It is definitely not pleasing to listen to that garbage.

There are moments in life that can be pretty scary. Sliding down a hill in your car on ice is anything but a pleasure trip, believe me. Having a bad dream is another example. Living a life of uncertainty in which you don't know where the next morsel of food is coming from or how you are going to meet your bills must be pretty frightening.

And consider those who are destitute. Many of us have no idea what it means to be pretty poor or pretty lonely or both. Certainly these conditions are not attractive, nor are they ever so pretty. Instead, we are blessed. May we always be mindful of that.

June 8, 2006

Just Not There!

I imagine by now students are now beginning to feel the pressure of being back at school and are buckling down and really working their tails off.

On the other hand, being that human beings never had tails to begin with, it is hard to imagine working something off that one never had to begin with.

I can hear now those who believe in evolution crying out, "Not so fast Pee Vee. We came from apes and they had tails." Sorry folks, but I do not follow that theory and stick by the philosophy of creationism.

In any case, I wonder how that expression ever came to be. I tried to find an Internet web site that could provide me with an explanation, but all that I found pointed me to people who were working very hard to accomplish a goal.

When I was in high school, I remember dancing to a song called "Shake a Tail Feather." The name of the singer escapes me at the present time. Have you ever seen tails with feathers on them on anything other than birds? Since humans don't have tails, there would be no way on earth we could ever dance displaying our plumage while doing robotic twists with our tails swinging to and fro.

I guess the same idea applies when someone says, "I worked my butt off to get that paper written." At least we know everyone has one of those. I hate to think what would happen if we worked so hard, it would fall off. Heavens to Betsy!

When it comes right down to it, we use some really strange expressions as part of American heritage. I don't even call it English, because that would imply the so-called sayings come from England (which they could have, I guess).

We seem to use the word "butt" in our expressions. "Butt" does not always refer to our posterior or as some may refer to them as our back end, but other usages as well.

For instance, carpenters who may be laying flooring will often butt two pieces of wood together before gluing them in place. I could understand if the back ends of each piece would be stuck together. Then the usage would make sense. But when these professionals butt the two pieces of wood together, they are doing so usually by joining the wood side by side.

A fellow Latrobean was telling me recently that he was disgusted with the fact that along the sidewalk near a park bench in the downtown area of our fair city there were cigarette butts all over the place. I told him wherever there were seats, you were bound to find butts (of course, it was a little play on words, so to speak). In my opinion, if a cigarette can have a butt, then who is to say that other objects can't also have them, too. That could include boots, pens, staplers, hammers, you name it. If two-sided objects have a front and a back with some kind of middle to it, I can only presuppose that the back end has to be labeled a butt, plain and simple.

I can't tell you how many times I have heard, usually women, yelling at their husbands, "When are you going to get off your butt and do something around the house?" That is one command I understand even though the Mrs. never quite put it to me that way. It's sad when spouses neglect to do responsibilities that obviously need to be done (but that is a whole 'nother column).

Animals will butt heads or horns when they get rammy (or moosey, elky or deery).

The larger or thicker end of anything is called a butt, according to my dictionary. It is also a thick part of a tanned hide of leather or a large end of the loin in beef.

It sure becomes clear to me by now that such a reference book has broadened my understanding of the many definitions and usages of the four-letter word.

But even though you may have some inkling of how some of the above-mentioned expressions may have started, there is still one that somehow doesn't fit into any of the usages given above.

Have you ever entered into a disagreement or tried to break up a fight whereby someone lashed out at you screaming at the top of his lungs, "Butt off, would ya?" Others may shout, "Butt Out!" None of us would relish being the recipient of such a comment. Nonetheless, we would rather hear this verbiage than one that contains four-lettered expletives!

November 9, 2006

NOT ANYMORE

When a friend came into my store not too long ago, we briefly shared opinions about this and that. When he was about to walk out the door, he blurted out, "Why don't you do a story on "Isn't anymore?"

Now, most of the time, when people come up and ask me to do columns on various subjects, I typically tell them, "If God doesn't guide me to do it, I usually don't." But somehow, I felt compelled to give it a try, relying on Him again for wisdom.

Throughout the many years I have had this machine (the computer), I have gotten emails stating "Remember the 50's?" or "Things you just don't see anymore," or the like. If one wanted to take the easy road to write about these topics, one would copy something that arrived via the Internet and transfer it to this tabloid.

Instead, I opted to use a completely different approach in considering "Isn't Anymore."

Let's start with the word *is*. This wonderful verb removes all doubt. It reveals fact. If you don't believe in it, then you are swayed by the power of this word and its suggestion of certainty.

Isn't declares non-existence, void, an absolute vacuum. Nothingness sums up this word. Even the dictionary defines the word as "Is not." That bothers me. Here is a word that if broken apart represents both the positive and negative in a matter of four letters.

How can lawyers ask when interrogating people in court, "Isn't it true that you . . ." There is nothing to support substantiation. I can only conclude that the usage, as "we and the attorneys" employ, creates an element of uncertainty.

On the other hand, in studying foreign languages, the word is used similarly throughout the world, so it can't be just "an American thing."

71

So, it is my observation that when someone states something *isn't anymore,* he is suggesting what was, really is not now. Confusing to say the least!

Now I must confess there are four other words that people seem to use loosely that drive me crazy. They are *can, will, could and would.* Can and could spell out acts of mechanical actions. Will and would are emotional drives governed by the mind. One must be very careful on using these words or risk the possibility of misspeaking.

For example, I was in my store one summer day when a chap walked in and greeted me. Seeing what I had on, he raised his eyebrows and exclaimed, "How can you put on those winter pants this time of the year? My reply was simple. "I grab the top of the pants with two hands. I first put my left leg into the left pant leg. Then I put the right leg into the right pant leg. Finally, I then pulled up my trousers."

"That's not what I meant," he commented as his facial expression showed his disapproval of my smart-allecky attitude—something for which I'm known.

But really. I was just answering his question as he had asked. If he would have said, "Why would you wear those pants in the summer time when it is so hot outside?" I may have responded, "It's like this—I keep putting off doing my laundry."

I elaborated, "One day, I looked into the closet and low and behold, there were no summer clothes, just winter ones. I had just one choice. It was either wearing the pants I have on, or going without pants all together. Aren't you glad at least I used enough brains to slip into something that is suitable for the occasion, as opposed to showing up for work in my swim trunks?" That not only got a smirk on his face, but a right-to-left constant head motion. I can only imagination what was going through his mind at the time.

So, if I suggest that you think before you speak, will you heed to a little advice? To my way of thinking, nothing that I have said will get you to change your ways in all probability. On the other hand, I did make you ponder a bit, didn't I?

September 21, 2006

On Life's Little Challenges . . .

DEAD-RINGER

Recently, while watching television, I happened to come upon a program where I observed one woman questioning another, "Hey, do you recognize me? Weren't you in high school with me? Weren't we in the same class?" The other woman had a mysterious stare on her face. I don't know if it was an expression of disbelief, or something of memory failure. In any case, one woman was very certain the two had crossed paths; while the other had no recollection of ever seeing the other.

A good number of years ago, I was told that there are seven other people in this world that look exactly like we do.

Off and on, I remember people coming up to me at different times and telling me they had seen me at different places or even on TV. Twice I was told I resembled two other photographers, one from Jeanette, and the other, God forbid, a fellow who took pictures for Playboy magazine.

I even was questioned one day about my television appearance. "Hey!" someone exclaimed. "You're the guy I saw on that talk show last night." Of course, he couldn't remember what show that was, and I convinced him it wasn't yours truly.

When we were in St. Louis in September, we rented a car from an agency. My son wanted to have the very best for me since it was my birthday getaway, so he informed the company that he wanted the best car available. This reservation was made three weeks in advance.

Upon arriving at this place of business, Aaron announced we were here to get the vehicle we had reserved. A gent came out and showed us what we would be renting. My wife proclaimed, "Surely, Brad Pitt, you can do better than that!" With that, we not only got a better car, but a 10 percent discount as well!

Did you ever walk up to someone thinking you were talking to an acquaintance or a friend of a friend, only to find out later, it was *not* the person you thought it was?

This happened to me back in the 60's when I was in high school. It so happens that I was somewhat attracted to one of my sister's friends, a twin. If ever there were two girls that looked precisely alike in every form and fashion, it had to be these two.

Well, stupid me, I decided to mosey over to the *wrong* young lady and fill her ears with personal mish-mush. When I found out later, I had tried to impress the twin's sister, it was one of the most embarrassing moments of my life.

Last summer, my wife and I drove to Pittsburgh to see an exhibit. Parking was limited, but we did find a lot. As we pulled in, we stared at the guy inside the booth. My wife asked the guy taking the money, "Has anybody ever told you that you look like Lynn Swann?" His answer:—"Everybody."

And of course, the most popular look-alikes that caught the world by surprise recently were Sarah Palin and Tina Fey. Even though I am definitely not a "Saturday Night Live" fan, I did happen to watch a small segment of the program where a gentleman walked up to Sarah thinking he was talking to Tina. You can imagine his embarrassment after he found out the truth, just as I did back when I was in high school, when I learned I had been talking to the wrong girl.

September, 2008

ALL GREEK, HUH?

I have yet to understand why the Greek language is the one picked on when someone does not understand a subject or a statement made to him.

The other day, I got a letter in the mail. Upon opening it, I could see right away that most the stuff in black print was far above anything this feeble mind of mine could fathom. So, I called the party from whom I got the letter and asked her to explain what all this mumbo jumbo was all about. I told her it was *all Greek to me.* She explained in a very nice way that the notification should have been sent to another family member and not me. I guess that made me feel a little better. At least this was one problem I could mark off my list.

Imagine standing in line waiting to get a ticket. A conversation is being overheard from the party in front of me. I shake my head and turn to my wife and state, "It's all Polish to me." That's the same as using the nationality *Greek*, isn't it? Would it be offensive to use any other country language other than the one previously mentioned?

I know people who live in this country may think that we speak *English,* but really it's American. We have our own way of talking as do they. A matter of fact, New Zealanders definitely speak *English.* I know because my sister is married to a Kiwi.

So, what was the origin of this famous expression? As in many of the other lines we have adapted in our everyday usage, we can owe our thanks to William Shakespeare. Taken from the tragic play, *Julius Caesar,* this expression occurs during a conversation between Casca and Cassius, two conspirators against Julius Caesar. The pun comes from the fact that a Romantic senator, Cicero, is speaking Greek and his fellows don't understand him. Thus, you now know the rest of the story.

Screwing on my thinking cap, I began meditating on all the applications.

Let's take products for example. Since many of the things we have in our households nowadays come from China, why not employ the name *Chinese* where we use *Greek*.

If we are reading the instructions of a product made in that country and we can't seem to understand how we are supposed to put it together, wouldn't it make sense to say, "It's all Chinese to me?" My keyboard is made there. It even has Chinese symbols underneath. Who in his right mind would want to refer to the Greek when the Chinese are responsible?

I have an old, black Swingline stapler. It was made in Long Island City, New York. I can't say *it is all Greek to me* what staples I should buy for proper usage. Instead, it only makes sense that I should insert the name American.

Some of the recipes that are found in health publications drive me crazy. They sound so very good to eat, and the author even brags how great the meal may taste. But, by looking at some of those ingredients, where does one find that stuff? It's all _____ to me (pick the language that matches the recipe).

And just mention the word *recipes,* have you ever been in a restaurant and you were brought something that looked most excellent on the menu, only to try to figure out what you are eating? You definitely can't blame the Greeks for this one, at least I don't think so. All that spicy, mixture of food in rolled up dough, is *all Spanish to me!*

And when it comes to the finest of wines, I immediately think of France. That's kind of funny, because I don't drink. Anyway, in my mind, I can hear Frenchmen holding up their glasses of Alsace or Le Bernat and pronouncing it with no trouble at all. People, who don't indulge, me included, may have a hard time stating each name correctly. To my way thinking, *it is all French to me*.

In my opinion, habits are easily formed if we don't give much thought as to usage of vocabulary. Just because Shakespeare started something doesn't mean we have to carry on the tradition, but it's not a bad reason to either. And if any baker from Greece spoke about his bread, *this would be all Greek to me!*

March 2, 2007

KINDA CRAZY!!!

Back in 2008 (seems like a long time ago), I was shooting the breeze with a friend of mine from church, when he looked over in my direction and quietly stated in a low tone, "When I turned 52, my whole world turned around. I felt and acted differently and I noticed a change within me," he said. "That's interesting," I told him. "When I was 64, I felt one way, but when I became 65, something changed within me." He followed by making a noise that sounded like "Hmm . . .," and I did the same. And that was the end to that short reflection of thoughts.

I have to wonder, after what this fellow told me, that maybe there is something to what we briefly discussed. I bet each senior can tell another the age the changing of the gears took part within him, moods changed, and what we took for granted, is no longer.

Just the other day, I filled my pill container. I did so just before taking my medication for the evening. Stupid me couldn't remember if I had taken the ones I needed to swallow already or needed to plop them in my mouth before retiring. Why is it that I spend so much time looking for a particular shirt to put on only to find it on my person already? Have I lost my sanity?

Back in the early weeks of deer season, I spent the entire day on the telephone calling deer processors concerning deer kills. I then wrote my "Inside the Outdoors" column and sent it off to the newspaper. Since I had been using my computer glasses for all my work, I never gave any thought to where my wire rims were. I just wanted to finish the story and move on to the next. I bet you know what's coming. You guessed it. I couldn't find my regular glasses anywhere. I looked for a better part of an hour and still nothing—on the table beside my bed, under the bed, on my dresser, in the bathroom and even on my computer stand. They were nowhere to be found. I thought to myself, "This is kinda crazy. I know they are here someplace." So, I thought of St. Anthony, the wonderful person who seems to know where absent-minded souls such as me seem to mislay things. No sooner did I think of him when, presto, I turned to my left, and one foot away from my arm was my spectacles. Go figure. Now, I'm starting to ask myself, did this happen to me when I was 52 or 64? Don't ask me to remember. That's impossible.

Word has it that when I go shopping now, I should make out a list so I won't forget to buy anything. Most the time I forget the list, so what good is it lying on my desk, now tell me? I've even put notes or other things I have to take to places in certain clothes, thinking they will be there when I get to my destination. What happens? I decide in the last minute to change my clothes, forgetting all together that the articles and what-have-you are contained in my clothes in the closet.

Here's a common problem that continues to blow me away. Why is it, when I'm writing a story, I bring to mind one word and end up typing something completely different? For example, I could be conveying, "Scott was the mentor for his son." But my brain wants me to type, "Scott was the mention for his son." What's happening here? Is being 65 really a reality of change or is it an age someone picked out of a hat? I'm starting to wonder. Maybe I should revert back to Wheaties and stop eating Cheerios.

March 19, 2009

Wait Just One Minute!

It was my day off. A matter of fact, it was a day of rest for many Americans. The annual holiday was Labor Day. Most of us welcome it because it is one of several weekends where there is that extended time to relax, have picnics or do things such as laundry we have been putting off for days on end.

This day was special for me. My wife did not have to work and so we decided to take a trip and go to our old stomping grounds at Cook Forest and enjoy the sights.

So, we piled a few things in the car and headed toward Indiana to pick up our daughter and her boyfriend. Along the way, my wife thought of some things we ought to take, so we stopped at one of the large outlets along the way. I told her I would stay in the car while she quickly ran in to purchase what she thought we needed.

I was at peace. I pushed the reclining bar down at the side of the car seat and felt the back drift into a laid back position. It was so nice to be away from home, particularly the noise of the traffic, not to mention the motorcycles.

Now, don't get wrong. I don't have anything against motorcyclists or motorcycles themselves. It's the noise they make especially when the rider accelerates to high rates of speed that is annoying. Heck, when I am trying to talk to my neighbor, one of these things comes by and I end up lip reading instead. Haven't gotten the hang of that just yet!

Anyway, getting back to the subject at hand, there I lay—blue sky and power wires above, and shoppers arriving all around, putting their blue bags into the cars or trucks. One chap beside me climbed into his vehicle just as I was lowering my seat and I decided to greet him a friendly hello. "Top of the morning to you," I said. "How ya doing?" was his response. That age-old response has been around for a long time. He lit up a cigarette, turned on his radio, started up his engine and put his gear in reverse. Quickly he pulled back, changed the gear to drive and headed up the hill. Another car pulled in his spot. The people got out and headed into the store. Things were at peace again (so I thought).

All of a sudden, the alarm goes off in the car beside me. Gad zooks! Rattle frattle! Zing zong!!! What happened to my peace and quiet? Sitting up in my seat, I looked all around. I thought the swat team was going to come out of nowhere and surround the vehicle with guns drawn and rifles pointed in hopes that they could capture the culprit who caused my day to go from calmness to calamity. I thought if I hide down underneath the dash, maybe they will think I didn't try to break in to this car. So I just sat there mystified.

This annoying sound went on and on and on. "How in the hay do I shut this thing off?" I thought. The driver had no way of knowing the agony he had caused me. I was going nuts on my day off. Great!

Wait just one minute. There has to be a solution to all this anguish. Should I have left a note on this guy's windshield telling him he just ruined my day? What good would that have done? With every passing moment, I was being tortured. Maybe I should have screamed. Then someone would have come over and helped me overcome this stressful situation.

Then all it once, it ceased. I know God sensed my need and told the car, "Enough!" and the vibration ceased. All I could think to say was, "Thank you, God, thank you, Jesus, thank you all the angels and saints, thank you guardian angel . . ."

But then, five minutes later it started back up. "Hey God, what are you trying to teach me here?" So, I weathered the storm the best I could, not blowing the car up as I felt compelled, not banging on its hood as a crazy person might, but just being relaxed, sitting in our car enjoying part of the day in a little different light, realizing that coping was part of tolerance. Maybe that was the lesson I was to grasp. This was just one of the many facets of labor. The day proved its worth with lessons as well as relaxation. Sometimes we want only good without recognizing the fact that challenging moments also have their place. But it must be understood, we can't move forward in life's journey unless we are open to growth by things that upset us. It's these learning mechanisms that are "potholes" to maturity.

September 16, 2010

On Animals . . .

It's Him!!!

Usually on my wife's day off, it has become the custom that we drive up to Indiana and spend the day with her mother or sister and family taking care of whatever needs arise. July 3, 2008 was one of those days.

We left our residence around 1:30 p.m. and headed toward our destination. A couple blocks down the road, I mentioned to my wife, Teri, that I had forgotten to purchase the Latrobe Bulletin, and asked if we could stop so that I buy the latest edition. So, she motored to the publishing company. I jumped out, hastened inside, dropped my 35 cents in the dish, grabbed a newspaper and got back in the car, and we were on our way.

We traveled on Industrial Boulevard eventually arriving at St. Rt. 217. We then ventured into Derry, as usual. As we made the sharp left hand turn it didn't take long to ascend up the bridge that extended over the railroad tracks below. We glanced briefly at the demolition of the building on the left and commented about the progress being made.

No sooner did we get to the bottom of the hill did we notice something out of the ordinary. Just before Teri made a right turn toward Blairsville we saw a small, dark brown dog with a pug nose running in a confused manner onto St. Rt. 217, and then across the road into a neighbor's yard.

"Quickly!," Teri yelled, "Get out the classified section in the paper and see if anyone lost a dog. It looks too nice to be a stray, and I think it's lost!"

So I did as told, and sure enough, under the "Lost" category was a dog matching its description to a tee—"A Boston Terrier Pug. Black w/ brindle, white chest, male, answers to Mokey." So my wife turned around the car and we went looking for it. At first we couldn't find it anywhere. Then out of the corner of my eye I shouted, "It's him! There he is running up the sidewalk on the bridge."

We headed up along the pavement and caught up with the animal. When my wife stopped her car, she put on her blinkers. I called the dog to come to the car. At first it looked at me unsure what to do. But then it decided to respond to our call.

Mokey first went out into the street and wanted to get in on Teri's side. When it figured that wouldn't work, he came around to my door. Now, I know I shouldn't have done it, but I picked up the animal and put it in the back seat of our car. I could sense it was really a loveable dog, so I chanced it.

I could hear someone yell from ten cars back, "Hey, he's taking that dog," as if that was supposed to scare me.

Anyway, the wife drove down to Rite Aid where we parked, and I called the owner using my cell phone. A man answered and I explained the story and that I had his dog. He put his daughter on the line. To say that she was overwhelmed with happiness was an understatement. The ironic thing was that she was shopping in Latrobe, and she and the dog lived in Derry. I was told they would be right over.

While waiting for the pair to arrive, we figured the dog must be thirsty, so my wife gave it some water from the car's cup holder. Mokey licked it dry.

Before long, a woman in a van pulled up beside our vehicle and jumped out with the biggest smile on her face. I opened the door and the woman took the dog in her arms and gave it lots of hugs calling it by name and expressing her gratitude all the while.

We later learned that Mokey belonged to her mother who had just moved to Derry from Ohio and recently became hospitalized. It had chewed its collar off three days before and escaped. The woman had put the ad in the paper the day we found him.

I praise God for putting us in the right place at the right time. It may have gotten injured or killed on that busy road if we hadn't have come along when we did.

July 17, 2008

Doing Its Thing!

Imagine if you can.

It's a warm, summer morning. The sun has just risen. You have just climbed out of bed and are looking forward to a brisk walk during the early hours before going to work.

You put on those exercise clothes that you set aside for your routine outing. Then, it's out the door and you are on your way.

The air is still cool, not to mention refreshing. Silence fills the air. Very few cars are motoring down your street. Occasionally, you can hear birds communicate with various tones and whistles that are ordinarily drowned out by mid-morning noises of high-powered engines, screaming kids, and loud, blaring radios.

As you hasten along your habitual path, you encounter squirrels playing in neighbors' yards, paperboys throwing daily tabloids onto porches, and dogs barking to be let in.

Two blocks up the street, you greet one gent who is walking his dog. You know you are on schedule because the two of you meet at the same place frequently.

Further along your travels, you eye the big hill. This is the true challenge of the morning. Can your pace time be broken? Do your strides lengthen propelled by the muscles in your legs, or do you walk normally, feeling little pain? The question goes through your mind. Should an attempt be made to set a new record or stay with the old one? A decision is made. Since the air is cool and comfortable, why torment oneself? After all, the briskness should suffice.

You get to the top and feel relieved that the incline is behind you. There is nothing but straight stretch ahead for about a mile before more grades become challenged goals. Psychologically, relief calms your innermost being.

Walking alone, you watch caretakers pull up to residences, people fetching newspapers, and workers warming up their cars for departures.

Here is where it gets good.

You round a corner, proceeding half way up the street, when all at once you notice a gray rabbit sitting in the middle of the sidewalk with a red collar around its neck. What is the first thing that enters your mind?

"Oh my gosh, someone's rabbit's gotten lose! What should I do? It's six o'clock in the morning. Should I start knocking on doors and ask neighbors if their pet rabbit escaped?"

You end up perplexed, right? After all, if the residents picked this morning to sleep in after staying up into the wee hours of the morning, their terminology might be a bit uncouth if you were to get them out of bed.

Can't you just imagine someone yelling at you? "What in the____do you think you are doing waking us up at this time of the morning? Are you some crazy wacko or something?" Their sour dispositions override your good intentions.

Other thoughts go through your head. What if a hawk, dog, or other predator kills this pet? Wouldn't you feel awful for not contacting someone? Maybe the bunny would wander out onto the road and get run over by a car. Just think, you could have prevented its death. Guilt sets in. You pause a few moments, but decide to move on. All peace by this time has left you.

You continue on your stroll down the street looking back occasionally to see if the animal is all right.

Moments later, about a block away, you encounter a man putting out his garbage. Relieved, you sigh all the time stating, "I just came down Spring Street and noticed a gray rabbit with a red collar sitting on the sidewalk. Do you suppose that is someone's pet that has escaped from its cage?"

Downplaying any alarm, the middle-aged homeowner says, "Oh, it didn't escape. Every morning about this time, the owners let the rabbit out of the house to do "its thing" and then it is called back inside."

Just think. You were about to knock on doors and wake up the neighbors. The nerve of you!

June 3, 2001

COME TO MAMA

Everybody values something. Some of these things have become status symbols, including cars, coins or artwork.

But what I'm going to talk about today is of different "nature." It has to do with status symbols of deer. Now, I can just hear someone thinking to himself, "Paul, what is this doing in the "Off the Wall" column and not the "Inside the Outdoors?" Simple. After reading a wonderfully written article in the 2009-2010 PA Hunting and Trapping Digest by Game Commission's Wildlife Biologist Jeannine Tardiff Fleegle, in a story titled "Where Do Baby Deer Come From," I thought I'd throw my twist into a story, using some of the facts taken from her story which was very informative.

I decided to interview a buck and get its comeback on a number of issues, including the stresses and some of the highs and lows it experiences between spring and fall. Here goes:

"Hi there, I'm Delbert. I was chosen by Paul to tell my story," he started to explain. "As a buck, I get very stressed out this time of year. In spring I have to grow antlers or the girls won't find me attractive. They don't see me for what I am. All they are impressed with are the horns on my head. What a bummer," Delbert said. "I have a wonderful body. I eat well. I think I am very masculine in appearance, and those does are attracted to my antlers? Go figure."

"Now, Paul, I have to also point out, the horns I carry around on my head aren't just to attract the females, but we also use them to communicate to both bucks and does. I make noise by rubbing my antlers on trees. We also use them to spar with the competition. What do you think of that—special, huh?"

"O.K., Delbert," I decided to question him, "When do you meet your counterpart for the long awaited 'coming together act' you prepared for back in the spring?" "In November," he told me. "The first two weeks of the month, does are pursuing me. Hey, it was nice to think back in the spring that I may find my woman, but when the first couple of weeks of the month roll around, there are literally thousands of girls looking to mate, possibly one with me. That certainly ups the spirits of any guy. They only have 48 hours to find their man, so stress enters their life, too," he divulged. "In the quiet of the forest during that time period, when the breeze is gently making its way through the treetops, keeping our ears in tune, we bucks just may hear the words, 'Come to mama,'" he asserted.

"I've seen many of my brothers and sisters scurrying about in a helter-skelter manner during these two days. It's a crying shame, because some of them aren't careful and run out on the roadways and get hit by vehicles and are killed. But you know, Paul," he said, "I may not come in contact with the girl of my dreams. She may be in one place, and I am here looking for her, and we may never meet in that short order of time. Talk about being stressed out. And you think, at times, you've got it bad. We also face disappointments," Delbert said.

"And you know something else, Paul?" "What's that," I asked. "After all my pursuits, and trying to find my woman, I lose 25 percent of my body weight. Can you get a load of that?" he blurted out. "Now, I guess I'm going to have to start eating more to build myself back up. Oh, and by the way, that beauty of a rack I had? I'll be losing it soon," he told me. "Dear me, this is the third year I have to grow a new one. That is, if a hunter doesn't get me first. Oh my, just another stress factor." Delbert emphasized, "If all goes well and I can avoid hunters, maybe I will find my girl next fall and we will then have kids next spring. I certainly am looking forward to having a family! I bet you have seen fawns running around in the open fields playing amongst themselves, having a good ol' time. That makes us parents mighty happy to bring into this world, children, who will grow up and enjoy everything that God, our creator, has given us. Instinctively, He has blessed us in many ways and we know we can count on Him for our many needs in the future," he concluded.

Sept. 12, 2009

How about Phyllis?

It's been said that behind every good man is a good woman.

If that's the case, then Punxsutawney Phil must have a lady friend hiding in its midst somewhere about the scene. After all, no man should be without a mate, regardless of breed.

After learning not too long ago that Phil saw his shadow on that winter Friday morning, I began thinking how lonely it must be for that most beloved critter to be penned up all year without rubbing noses with the opposite sex.

Just suppose there is a Phyllis we know nothing about. What kind of life does she have? After all, her male counterpart gets all the attention, and she remains completely in the background.

In the past, we have had many statesmen and presidents whose wives stayed out of politics and went about their duties in a respectable manner. Consequently, it is easy to surmise that Phyllis must lead a rather interesting life if there is such an animal.

Let's just pretend that this furry female is in the picture, so to speak. Wouldn't man want to make the two of them as comfortable as possible? When you think of it, we are dealing with a celebrity here, so the little woman should be treated with a great deal of respect, too.

It is my belief that she should be pampered, petted, and groomed just as much as her hubby. If the woman of the house is given tender care, then her feeling will be extended to her man, and both will live in a loving household.

On the other hand, take our girl out of the house, and all we have is a lonely old man who is exposed to the public once a year for a few minutes for the purpose of carrying out a tradition. Granted, it has roots as a Christian holiday called Candlemas. Nevertheless, it seems a shame that so much emphasis is put on a certain date in February with the consequence that after the animal makes its appearance, it is pushed back into its quarters not to be seen again until a year later.

At least if Phyllis was there, he may feel better about the whole thing, smiling to the crowd, looking around and viewing his shadow, waving to onlookers, and then heading back to his waiting spouse in the confines of "home sweet home."

Can't you just hear her say, "Phil honey, you were spectacular! Did you see how the people looked at you? Can't you tell they really love you, too? I'm so proud of you!"

Now, doesn't that beat being pushed into a dark cubicle with bars on the front gate and caged in there, alone, to look out at a bunch of "crazies" jumping around, doing a bit of a jig, and cheering and shouting?

Phil has to have a mate he can call his woman.

Who's to say groundhogs don't get depression? If I were Phil, I'd get on some kind of mood lift to get myself out of the dumps. It goes without saying that prayer would definitely be of great asset, but I don't think this form of communication has been introduced to these creatures.

Granted, this great Pennsylvania resident does go on tour prior to the big event. I'm not sure his spirits are raised on these excursions, though. Now, if Phyllis was with him, that might be different.

"Look dear," she would say. "There's Mr. Bush, our newly elected President." Of course, Phil would probably just grunt and give her a half-hearted smile. If this was his first trip to the President's home, he may feel differently, but it seems journeys always follow the same path. How exciting can one be after visiting the White House once a year for the last 20?

Look at it this way. Sharing is a wonderful way of life. Whether it be around the dinner table, looking for food together, as Phil and Phyllis may do, or visiting neighbors for a chat or two, togetherness is necessary.

I know what many of you are thinking by now. If cohabitation is permitted, problems will definitely spring forth. What then? I'm not sure I have the answer to that, but, on the other hand, I know something can be worked out.

So, what's to come of all this? Probably nothing. It was just a thought. My mind works that way sometimes.

March 10, 2000

On Encounters . . .

CLYDE

Everyone who saw him sitting against the wall was aware this character was not cheerful. It was almost as if he was depressed and there was nothing one could do to pull him out of it. Even his family members had doleful looks giving observers the feeling it must be a family trait.

Day after day, one would pass, sometimes taking note of the senior member. Other times, people would walk by, pretending he didn't exist. That's just the way it was with Clyde.

One day, I decided to pull up a chair and just watch him. Many things went through my mind. As Clyde looked down with a sad expression on his face, I wondered how many others shared the same posture.

The first thing that entered my mind was, I bet they were sad because no one had given them their yummy-tummy treats, and it was way past the time they were to get them.

Or, maybe they were in their doldrums because of having to wait a full seven hours or so before they could hop to it and play ring-around-the-rosy in the middle of the floor? I had no clue, and could only sit there and wonder.

Just looking at Clyde filled my mind with all kinds of questions. There was definitely mystery about him.

As he sat there looking with glasses resting on his nose, I could not but wonder what was really making him tick. I then started thinking about the younger generation and what was on their mind. To say I was awe struck was to put it mildly.

I began to sense that maybe Clyde had a disease, and his declining health was starting to get the best of him. Problems like that often tend to throw people into slumps. Could it be that this fellow had a disabilitating disease, and his family was outwardly depressed about it? Sometimes, there never exists answers.

But to this story, there is an uplifting twist.

95

Even though Clyde seems down in the dumps all the time, he is deeply loved by children and adults alike. Many times, youngsters passing by will greet him. Periodically, adults have tried to persuade others to take him home with them. It was not unusual that such attention became a daily affair.

Actually, Clyde found a genuine touch of love extended his way quite often. But it mattered not. His facial features always remained the same.

So, what was so special about this little guy? He draws kids to himself, is loved and hugged, has a definite appeal to most who come in contact with him, yet never cracks a smile. Could Edison, Jefferson, Einstein or Chaplain ever have received such attention?

The answer is "no." For you see, Clyde is not a human being at all, but a stuffed basset hound that sits in the waiting room of Johnson Family Eye Care, 600 Ligonier St., Latrobe. The glasses that are seen on its head were placed there to advertise the business product.

Just seeing someone's creation tripped my mind into a line of thought I never expected. All kinds of ideas accompanied by imagination flashed in front of me. As an adult, I felt pulled down into a world of gloom and loss of hope. My sensitivity to Clyde's expression had negative value.

To children, however, looks mean nothing. They see hope and love in everything despite appearance.

If only we adults could hold onto the many treasures children have, what a better world this would be.

July 21, 2001

FLIPPED HER TAIL

There I stood stranded. There was water all around me. I had located a small island after my boat had sunk after being splashed by a big wave while I was fishing a mile or two off the coast of Bar Harbor, Maine.

Thank God, I was able to lug my fishing rod, reel and some lures with me to this sandy turf where practically no life existed, except yours truly, and who knows what. If ever there was a feeling of despair, this was it.

People dream of exotic vacations. They get out books, contact travel agents or get on the Internet. Then they piece together plans step by step so their trips are ones they will remember. I think I did it backwards. I jumped in my boat, headed out into the waters and then let nature take its course. How was I to know such a revolting development was going to take place?

Being alone on an island particularly one with a small bit of ground, maybe three trees and a few rocks and dried wood, is not my idea of what I would plan for a get-away vacation. Nevertheless, I was stuck here and had to make the best of it.

Lots of things go through my mind when no one else is around. What would you do if you knew you were secluded out of sight of others? My first thought was get comfortable. Of course, how comfortable can one get on a protruding hunk of dirt being threatened by water splashing against the shore all around you?

The first thing I knew I had to do was get out of the wet clothing. All I needed was to get sick, and I sure didn't need that. So, I stripped down and hung my garments on tree branches so the rays of the sun would dry them.

Now, I have to admit, I am not one to march around in my birthday suit in public. On the other hand, how public could this place be, considering I was the only one there?

Instead of panicking, I decided to string up my rod and proceed to fish. There wasn't a whole lot to do. I thought I might as well get a bit of food stored up. I knew upcoming nourishment would not be three balanced meals.

As I stood there in the buff casting and retrieving my lure, I heard a faint summons of someone calling my name. Now, I knew that I had been on the island only a short time. Was the experience getting to me already? I heard my name called out a second time. "Paul, Paul, come over here. I want to talk to you."

I was taken aback to say the least. I almost went into a state of shock, but instead controlled my composure. Since I couldn't find a fig leaf to cover certain parts of my anatomy, I grabbed a piece of driftwood and carried it in front of me. I then went over to see who was calling. To my utter surprise, I discovered a mermaid waiting for me. Various things entered my mind. "Am I seeing things? There is no such thing as mermaids," I concluded. It was great to see another "person," though, but one with a flipper on her lower torso? I knew I now had someone to talk to. That spelled relief to some degree.

"Paul," she whispered. "You will never have to worry about food. I will make sure you have plenty," That was comforting. "And don't worry about your nakedness. I won't tell anybody," she said. I guess that statement eased my mind, even though it was a little difficult to swallow.

"I will return every so often and make sure you are all right," the aquatic brunette reminded me. Of course, she didn't detail how often that would be, but I knew I was in good hands (I guess). Could God have sent one of His creations to care for me?

The dazzling beauty turned back to the waters, flipped her tail and disappeared under the surface. When she would return would be anybody's guess.

God has gifted us all with imagination to one degree or another. In this little story, I definitely envisioned a fish-like female coming from the depths of the ocean, surprising me when I thought I was all alone. One could be somewhere else and let one's mind be a bit creative. I don't think that means we have lost our minds, or are taking drugs. It's just placing ourselves somewhere else just for a moment, or several minutes, as the case may be.

I have heard many times, "Imagine being on an island surrounded by beautiful women fanning you with palm branches . . ." What's so different about my little story than this. Take it as a fun thing to do, and then let it go.

You just may have enjoyed the moment!

June 3, 2004

Is that you?

After saying a little prayer before entering a nursing home, we entered through two double doors and proceeded to go inside. My friend and I decided to discuss whom we would visit that day. It was kind of a ritual by now.

Seeing a number of familiar faces, we greeted each by name, spent a few minutes talking to them, and then moved on. That was our approach, and we felt very comfortable with it.

No matter which way we went, long corridors appeared in front of us. As people of habit, we usually worked counter-clockwise, depending which facility we visited.

Sometimes my friend would visit one resident on one side of the hallway, and I, across the way.

So, here we walked, discussing whatever came to mind, when all of a sudden I hear a faint call, "Paul, is that you?" I stopped dead in my tracks. Two things crossed my mind. Nobody ever calls me Paul, and second, who would know me to greet me as such.

"Paul," a quiet speaking older woman called, "I'm over here. Come over and talk to me."

I turned and headed right toward the person who I believed was trying to get my attention. I walked right up to her. She displayed a great big smile on her face followed by an embarrassing question, "Don't you remember me?"

I had to be perfectly honest. I wasn't going to lie. I wanted to be tactful, but, on the other hand, I knew lying was a sin, so I knew I had but only one choice.

"I'm sorry," I said. "I know it's been a long time since I've seen you and my memory is not that good anymore." Maybe that was a white lie, maybe not. In any case, I thought I was doing what was right.

"Isabel, Isabel Jackson," she exclaimed.

"Oh, my gosh!" I blurted out. "It is so good to see and talk to you. It has been a long time."

"How are the kids," she asked. I'm always touched when people ask about our son and daughter. "They must be up in age now, and probably just as successful as their dad."

I wanted to give this lady a hug. I could sense the love coming from her heart. It was simply wonderful. There was no other way to describe it. She then wanted to know more about my life, and what I had done since I saw her last. It was simply a moment to treasure.

"How long has it been since I saw you last, do you think?" By the time we put our thinking caps on together, we figured out, we may have worked together briefly approximately 25 years ago at Kennametal in Latrobe. After that, I believe I saw her in church occasionally with her father, Albert, but only a number of years.

He was a wonderful man with a wealth of information. I remember encountering him one afternoon at a nearby lake. He loved to fish. Making spoons for that purpose was his favorite past-time pleasure. I watched him display his tactical maneuvers. When he cut loose one lure and changed to another, he would share his many fishing adventures. What a treat, to say the least.

There are a lot of Isabels and Alberts in nursing homes who need a loving touch, but rarely get visitors. Stopping by for 10 minutes, for example, can make a tremendous difference to those who may feel abandoned. God calls us to share His love with others.

Maybe if in the future, the Holy Spirit inspires you to visit someone confined to a bed, wheelchair or even to a residence, you may hear the words, "Is that you?" This just may be your cue to bring a ray of sunshine to those who have known only darkness.

August 16, 2007

MEETING MUFFET'S DAUGHTER

I was on my last leg of completing my usual jaunt. As I rounded the corner of our city block, I noticed a little girl in a sitting position eating out of a bowl. As I got nearer, I could see that she was concentrating on her task.

Now, everyone knows how much I love talking to people, no matter what their age, young, middle-aged, or senior citizens. So, it goes without saying that when I saw this youngster there, I felt compelled to talk to her.

"Aren't you the Muffet daughter?" I said.

At first, she did not look at me. I concluded that she was hungry and eating was foremost on her mind, and not making casual conversation. I was a kid once. I understand.

"Say, that's a pretty dress you are wearing," I commented. She turned from what she was doing and looked into my face. I then asked in a different way about her dad. "Isn't John Muffet your father?" She nodded and continued eating.

"Are you comfortable sitting on a tuffet?" was my next question.

"It's OK," she mumbled in a low tone. I could tell she wasn't thrilled about it, but positioned herself on it to eat her meal.

After conversing a bit more, I decided to call her by name. "Hey, Little Miss, what are you eating? That stuff doesn't look that great to me."

"Curds and whey. My mommy fixes it for me for lunch every day," she stated.

"Do you like that?" I had to quiz her. "It's not that bad. After eating it so long, I've gotten used to it," the blond-haired youth remarked.

During the course of our nice little chat about things, I noticed out of the side of my eye a spider in the grass. I then proceeded to warn her.

"Aaaaaa . . . Little Miss, what do you think about spiders?"

"Why, Pops?"

That answer took me by surprise, but then knowing my daughter calls me that instead of Dad, as an expression of endearment, I felt in the little amount of times we had spent together, it must be a term she also considers someone special.

"Well, there is one coming your way. If you don't like them, I don't want you to be alarmed." With that, she jumped up, clutching her clay container and scurried off, disappearing out of sight in no time at all.

I'm sure by this time you realize that the story you just read was fictional.

The fact that I was blessed with such a great imagination opens doors to writing stories not only about nursery rhyme characters, but making any inanimate object come alive. Thus, what you read resulted in how my brain puts occurrences in place.

But writing just how I met Little Miss Muffet was just the beginning. I wanted to further understand words that were used in the rhyme that were new to me.

So, I first started asking everyone who entered my store one day, "What were the first two lines of the nursery rhyme, 'Little Miss Muffet,' and what exactly was a 'tuffet'?" The majority of the people didn't know the one word in question.

After doing a bit of research, I was able to find out from the website: "Yahoo Reference Dictionary" on the Internet that a 'tuffet' is "a clump of tuft of grass, or a low seat such as a stool."

Next, I was curious as to what "curds and whey" were. According to Funk and Wagnall's New Comprehensive Dictionary, 1971 edition, "A curd is the coagulated portion of milk, of which cheese is made, as distinct from the watery portion or whey."

So when I asked my fantasy character how she liked her lunch on that one particular day, we can only suppose she was being polite by telling me it was all right.

I don't know. Maybe there are people who find this dish so. Some may consider it very tasty. As much as I love most food, I think I'll pass on these two!

June 1, 2002

And Then There Was Mildred

Recently, I had to go into downtown Latrobe to get some blood work done, so I visited Latrobe Area Hospital's clinic on Ligonier Street.

No sooner did I enter, then I was asked to come over to the information desk where a receptionist greeted me pleasantly.

After seating myself, I went through the usual questions-and-answers routine that everyone has to undergo before the procedures can be carried out.

I don't think I was in my chair for more than 15 seconds when I noticed a female subject nearby. Of course, it could have been a "him," but I liked to refer to my new acquaintance to my left as a her, don't ask me why.

She gazed motionless, staring at me. I was awestruck and peered at her wondering just what was going through her mind. It is not often that I get such a look, particularly from the opposite sex. It actually caught me by surprise.

Now, I could have introduced myself and her to me. That certainly would have broken the silence between us. Instead, I chose a name that I would keep in my mind. Sometimes, that works better if you can pick one out of a hat, so to speak, and assign it to a character, and then you can associate the imaginary identity with the real name.

It didn't take long for me to decide to call her "Mildred." Here again, don't ask me why I picked that name. She just looked like a Mildred, I guess, so that was the name I assigned to her.

I know I was slowing down the proceedings, but I had to pose what I considered a very important question to the girl behind the desk. "How did it come to be that this attractive female was positioned at your location?" I asked the hospital employee.

"Oh," the young lady stated, "one of the girls, who works in this department, thought she (Mildred) would add color to this place."

And that she did!

Now, you may be surmising that the female to which I am referring is a human being. But, I am sorry to disappoint you. The subject in question turned out to be a Betta, a small tropical freshwater fish, so I was told by Jim Gracie, owner of Aqua Pet on Main Street in Latrobe. This Thailand native was being kept in a round bowl with some colored marbles on the bottom and plant-life floating on the surface.

Thinking back what I was told concerning Mildred's presence, I wondered why anybody would put a purplish-black fish, no more than two and one—half to three inches in length in a see-through container, and claim that it would add color to the room.

In the remaining moments, I sat there just prior to signing my paperwork before letting the technician collect my blood, many questions went through my mind. What was Mildred thinking as she gazed through the curved-out structure? We people must have appeared really distorted from the convex glass. On the other hand, we must be pretty weird creations, anyway, to put big fish in little bowls. Do you think Mildred eyes visitors as twisted and bent out of shape as those who see themselves in wavy mirrors in carnivals?

Do you imagine Mildred wondering why she isn't given more attention than she gets?

After all, her family history goes back to the King of Siam in 1840. The Germans saw the species in 1896, and their move to America occurred in 1910.

Oh, but what have we done with this beautiful aquatic wonder—created a fad by sticking Bettas in a bowl. Consumers are advised when purchasing them that these fish should not be fed, or the water changed EVER.

That is nice . . . how humane. But not all hope is lost. Mildred has a chance after all. Isn't it fortunate "our girl" is in a hospital setting where the utmost of professional care can be expected to be given by the "roommates."

Changing the water twice a week, treating it and selecting proper foods will add to a "Betta-care facility."

Oh, Mildred, I am probably not the first guy at whom you stared, and I know I will not be the last. I can handle that.

Swim around and enjoy that little enclosure.

Think of it this way. At the present time, you just may feel better than the majority of the people sitting near you!

May 22, 2003

On Advice . . .

PMS

How often have you heard the expression, "It's easy? It's no big deal." Or, "I don't know why you are getting bent out of shape about it. It's a snap." Finally, "Hey, if I can do it, you can, too." Now that's all well and good for those who have properly been instructed to perform what they're supposed to carry out, but if you are like me, sometimes things just aren't as simple to carry out as others might suggest.

This brings me to the subject at hand—PMS. I want to assure you that those three letters do not stand for Patti and Mike Sherback, puffy midsection, or the common reference to Premenstrual Syndrome. Instead, the way I see it, the abbreviation stands for "Poor Me Syndrome."

I first thought about writing this column when my doctor put me on oxygen back in February, but for some reason, I decided to hold off. Then recently, two lovely ladies and I had a chat on the path in Legion Keener Park and one told me of a friend who would not leave her house because she needed to be on oxygen most of the time. It wasn't so much that she couldn't, I was told. It is more that she wouldn't. Of course the question arose, "Can you still do the things you used to do?" My response—"Not all of them, but I can still remain active and do quite a bit. I just can't do them as long, maybe."

I think the key response when facing adversity is to always keep one's sense of humor (if one has one), and not pity one's self. There are others far worse off than oneself, and by chance, if one were to visit them, one would quickly see that this new dilemma may be minimal compared to others.

I also believe we all can do something for others. When we were young or middle-aged, most of us had jobs, some very prestigious ones. Upon retiring, a number of adjustments had to be made. Some people have found these very difficult and have a similar mind-set as those who may have been stricken with a sudden illness or an accident leaving them disabled. But what some people fail to recognize, is that from the age one started employment to when one called it quits, God created a job source for one to provide food for the table and money to pay monthly bills. For those who are not working due to either of those reasons, God has passed on the message of sorts—"I helped you understand what you were to grasp in becoming gainfully employed. Now that you have more time on your hands, I would like it if you could spend more time giving it back to me." How easy is it to say, "I could have done more when things were better, but I can't do it now." I sense a bit of PMS.

When I had the privilege to chat with a middle-aged woman on a treadmill next to mine, while I was trying my hand at therapy at Excela Health Latrobe Area Hospital, she told me she was bored at home. In as much as she was on oxygen now, she could do very little. She added, her husband stays home and watches television most the time and takes short walks everyday. Believe me or not, when she told me this, I was disturbed. Right then and there, I wanted to start an organization to get people out of the house and doing something to help others and themselves even if it's minor. Not only would they be doing God's work, but they would get distracted from PMS.

Then I discovered that Westmoreland County Community College has just what the doctor ordered called RSVP—Retired and Senior Volunteer Program. It recruits volunteer and matches them with meaningful opportunities for service in nonprofit organizations. Those 55 years and older may participate. The program continually seeks out new volunteer opportunities in the areas of education, health and human needs, the environment and public safety. The great thing is it has something for everyone.

Whatever one's selection, RSVP volunteers provide more than just their skills and knowledge, they give their friendship—they give themselves. For more information and details, call 724-925-4213, or 1-800-262-2103, extension—4213. Serving God *is* serving others.

August 20, 2009

RUN SPOT!

Recently, I spent an incredible amount of time on the telephone with a technology representative concerning my Internet connections. There were periods of time that I needed to wait while he made some adjustments. As is often the case when waiting for an answer on the phone, I began to sing two of my favorite songs, "Row, Row, Row Your Boat," and "It's a Lovely Day in the Neighborhood." After finishing these songs, I typically ask the recipients of my singing if they have heard of Mr. Rogers and mention that I am calling from his neighborhood.

In this instance, this fellow told me he had never heard of our local legend, so I switched the conversation to something else and still invited him to sing "Row, Row, Row Your Boat" with me. As usually is the case, most people decline to sing and tell me they can't sing, or "You wouldn't want to hear me sing." I then tag on the comment, "God wants us to sing a joyful noise unto Him. He never said it has to be harmonious or in tune." Sometimes people will give it a go.

For some reason or other, not knowing his age, I asked the gent, "Do you remember Dick, Jane and Spot?" His reply was in the affirmative. I then knew we had something in common.

At a later date, I thought of our conversation, and wondered how the trio would fit into today's society, rules and regulations.

For example, you'd never see Dick or Jane down at Legion Keener Park in Latrobe with Spot. You'd never hear either of them yelling, "Run Spot, Run," because dogs aren't allowed down there. I then wondered if Spot ever saw a goose. Since they hang out down there along the Loyalhanna Creek, it would have been a real treat for him to chase after these birds—not that he would have been able to catch any of them or would have tried. I don't think Spot was that type of dog.

I can't imagine Spot ever being leashed. If he were, I think Jane would have gone flying through the air, being pulled behind him. Since my memory doesn't serve me right at my age, I can't recall if Spot was a male or a female, just a family pet. In any case, I also don't remember the command, "Just walk, Spot, walk." Spot always ran.

When I think of the family pet, what a wonderful life Spot must have had. The pictures I recall viewing always had him smiling. An animal that shows such expression is happy, well cared for and knows it is loved. That certainly must be a great feeling from an animal's point of view.

I don't recollect the command, "Spot, stay in the yard, stay in the yard!" It was always "Run Spot, Run!"

I can't imagine that this legendary pet was ever bad. I can only conclude he always responded to his owners as ordered to set good examples for children to obey their parents. Of course, how many mothers or fathers call out to their kids, "Run Andrew, Run," when scampering down the sidewalks of one's hometown or even in the cities. I think it's very much the other way, if you ask me. Parents want to keep their kids under control and usually try very hard to guide them for safety sake.

But, I'm not saying that there are no longer Spots around anymore. A lot of dog owners will throw Frisbees to their pets that will jump for them and bring them back to their masters. Canines that have been to obedience school are quick to act upon orders given, whether it be to heel, told to go after something, or to stay within property boundaries. Can you imagine Dick or Jane sending Spot to obedience school? Spot was a dog that always did everything right, that would go beyond the call of duty to fulfill the wishes of his masters. Maybe he didn't observe all the Ten Commandments, but he always gave total love to his masters and their friends, and received the same in return.

Here's a suggestion: If you are one of those folks who are not familiar with the stories of Dick, Jane and Spot, ask someone who knows about them. Then pass on the tales to the kids of today. I think it will be fun for them to hear the stories we grew up with when we were young.

October 16, 2008

BACK OFF!

Throughout the years I have lived in the city of Latrobe, I have met several couples, some with one or two offspring, and others with as many as eleven kids in the family. A matter of fact, right off the top of my head (under my hair), I know of three families in the greater Latrobe and Derry areas that had eleven children, some born into the nuclear family, and others adopted developing a blended family.

I remember when I had a store, one couple came in every year to purchase identification photos for the purpose of going to Russia to adopt 11 children from one family over a period of so many years. I admired that. Their objective was to keep the family together—and they succeeded.

Some of you may remember the 7th Heaven television series. Annie and Eric Camden had seven children. Now you may be saying, "That was only a TV show. It was just a stage performance, so in all likelihood it wasn't true at all." Probably not, but that's not to say people still do have large families about the size as the Camdens.

Take Edgar and Ethel Whoople. He fathered eight children, one more than Eric, and both Edgar and Ethel raised their children to love the Lord with all their hearts, honor their parents, and love the neighbors as themselves. They are very respectable, gentle children who always are in the best of behavior wherever they go or are seen. That not only speaks well for the Whooples, but how these kids were brought up as well.

Another such family that has nine kids are the Hooleys. I have come to admire Jacob and Henrietta and family as well. Each child, in the presence of the public, is "angelic." I've been among families with one to two children, and none can compare to the behavior of their offspring. A matter of fact, it's a whole different world when I am around the Hooley children. Do you think the parents waved a magic wand and presto, they became well-mannered individuals, or was it the combination of discipline and proper upbringing that was the ticket? What do you think? I have to believe it was the latter. No one can wave anything over a kid's head and expect miracles, except maybe in a healing ceremony.

So you see, there is something the Whooples and the Hooleys have very much in common, besides a deep love within each nuclear family that bonds them together. In addition, all the children in both families are very well groomed, always look neat from head to foot, wear clean, pressed clothing, and never, ever appear disheveled.

Recently I learned some disturbing news. Both families are being looked down upon wherever they go. Edgar told me when he took his children to the playground recently, a "gentleman" approached him and boldly stated, "Boy, you have your hands full! Are they all yours?" "No," the father replied sarcastically, "They belong to the milkman!"

What gives anybody the right to tell others what they can and cannot do? Doesn't the Holy Scriptures tell us, "Go forth and multiply?" It doesn't tell us to subtract once it gets to the sum of its parts, does it?

"Back off." If the Whooples, Hooleys or other families like them want to raise six, eleven or more children, and they have the means to do so, all the more power to them. If these two very loving couples feel led by the Holy Spirit to bring children into the world, they should feel free to do it.

For the general public to give these wonderful people evil stares is something only reflecting what is in their hearts is demeaning to say the least. If this column speaks to any of you that may be doing this very thing, I would recommend you change your ways and clean up your act, plain and simple.

You show me where it is written in the Bible, "Go forth and look down upon your neighbor, criticizing him for everything you couldn't have, failed to try to have, or are just plain jealous to those who may have something greater than you do." You aren't going to find it. If you do, it surely isn't in the Holy Scriptures, handed down by a loving God such as we know today.

Remember, love is like peanut butter. It always sticks when you spread on just a little bit.

May 14, 2009

Was It Abe?

I don't think I was much different than many of my high school cronies when we entered high school. Most of us knew we had four years ahead of us and that our challenges would be anything but easy. Nevertheless, we did our thing, going to classes, writing reports, taking tests and going the whole nine yards that go along with pubic education.

I can almost predict that few of us were thinking about college when we entered our ninth grade year. At that time, more important things were on our minds such as sports, dances, and need I say, girls. A matter of fact as we moved up the ladder to the higher grades, the attraction to the opposite sex captured my attention much more than subjects we were forced to take as part of what was referred to as the basic curriculum.

Thinking back, it is hard to recall just what subjects I had at the time? Can you recall yours?

Not believing that I was of the caliber to go to college, I sought the easy way out. I took the general courses just enough to graduate from high school. Looking back, I wish I would have paid a little more attention to the teachers of those courses. Most of the subjects dealt with bookkeeping, math, typing and basic English. I didn't consider the fact that I would have a store someday and everything that was being taught then would definitely be relevant to my endeavors today. Oh no . . . I thought I was playing it smart and cruising through four years just to graduate. To my way of thinking, I had no plans after commencement, so my interests were otherwise.

I paid for it later. After making through all four years and leaving high school behind, I ended up going to college preparatory school. I needed to take some basic courses to get into institutions of high learning. Taking the easy way out surely taught me a lesson.

But getting back to my high school alma mater, there was one class I hated. I blame it on the fact that the teacher and I had personality conflicts.

No matter what I did, I couldn't get the hang of history. At that time, I thought to myself, what a drag. Who would ever want to be interested in this "stuff" anyway? So what if certain people circled the globe in boats, battles were fought, and/or inventors, through tinkering and research, put together some tools that may still be used today. I could care less.

I think my teacher picked up on my attitude and graded me accordingly. On the other hand, if she would have been a little nicer to me and maybe made the subjects more interesting, I think I could have done better.

This whole introduction brings me to something I heard someone say the other day. A statement was made that Patrick Henry was the father of our country. Even though I flunked history, I knew that wasn't right. So, I decided to ask students and adults alike who visited my store. NO ONE customer knew the answer for sure, regardless of age. Some people even shrugged their shoulders as to say they didn't have a clue. That's sad to say the least. One high school pupil asked, "Was it Abe?" A couple others thought it might be Benjamin Franklin. I loved the answer given to me by one young fellow, "No one taught me when I went to school in Latrobe what I should know as a high school graduate!"

It all goes back to listening and wanting to learn, considering what is being taught as important and retaining it as useful information.

I did seek out a person in the know, who not only verified that George Washington is the father of our country, but also pointed out that the history lesson describing this topic is taught in fourth grade at Latrobe Elementary School. Could it be that our graduate was apathetic at the time of his lessons, or found himself a bit distracted by other avenues of thought when that very important part of history was being taught? What's done is done. No use digging any further into the past.

The moral of the story is this. If you are being taught something, listen. If you do not care for the topic, listen anyway. Retain as much as mentally possible. You will never know if you'll need that information sometime in the future. It is better to know the basics than to plead ignorance to those facts of which we all should be aware.

May 20, 2004

LIFT OFF

When I learned recently that one of the two most popular months to marry is right around the corner, I decided now would be the time to write this column.

Not too long ago, I emailed Latrobe photographer Keith E. Lewis, and asked him the question, "What is the most popular month to get married?" I was surprised to learn that there are two months, June and October.

Of consequence, I decided to dedicate today's "Off the Wall" to those who plan to tie the knot in a couple of weeks. To illustrate what goes on before and after the "big day," I will use the analogy of a rocket ship to a relationship for all intended purposes.

Let's begin by imaging this huge structure in an enormous warehouse. All the parts are assembled nearby ready to be put in the proper places in the space ship. Likewise, each part can represent persons all gathered in one room mingling together. Through the connection of one instrument to another, the unit comes together. With the interaction of one person to another, a relationship forms. As more components are joined together, the mechanism begins to take shape. As persons get to know each other better, chemistry unites an emotional tie. After a lengthy period of time, the ship is completed. Thus it is with people, a love has been created, visible to all.

The rocket is taken to the launch pad and set into place. Once the couple is ready for marriage, a ceremony takes place. There has been preparation for both the big days. Concerning the rocket, people will gather on the outskirts of Cape Canaveral and wait for its blastoff. Pertaining to the couple, onlookers will gather to watch their nuptial tie.

When lift off is announced, connections are disengaged from the ship. After marriage occurs, "A man shall leave his mother and a woman leave her home, and they shall travel on to where the two shall be as one," as

119

the Wedding Song goes. What is seen when the rocket leaves the pad are flames coming from its engines. What the two are feeling from within, are burning passions taking them forward in limitless directions.

As the shuttle is thrust forward into the wide open spaces, the newlyweds find themselves involved with each other, going on that special honeymoon where each will be able to enjoy the other in an unlimited unselfishness of love for each other.

But when the spaceship gets so high, something extraordinary happens. No longer does it stay as one unit. The booster rockets fall away and the shuttle thrusts forward to enter space. Such is life when the couple returns from the honeymoon and mainstream living sets in. If both are employed, each will return to his and her jobs. All the glamour of preparing for the wedding, going on the honeymoon, enjoying each other's company in a place far separated from the families is history, plain and simple.

As that plane enters a zone where there is no gravitational pull, its operation is dependent upon the knowledge of the astronauts who will steer the craft in the direction they want it to go. No longer will the new couple be playing house together. Each made a commitment on their wedding day, not only to the other, but to God as well, that they would "have and to hold, from this day forward, for better, for worse, for richer, for poorer, in sickness and in health, until death do us part." They must trust in God to help them from the day they announced, "I do," to every living day they spend together.

And as the space shuttle will spend its undetermined time in orbit, so will the couple be together, united by and with God as long as they adhere to biblical principles listed in Corinthians. These include patience, kindness, not showing jealousy, always seeking the other's interests, watching one's temper, and not rejoicing over wrong doing. Love "bears all things, believes all things, hopes all things, endures all things."

Just as a spaceship, each duo started out as a package deal. The aircraft may have been projected into the air with a hopeful destination. Married couples, too, should strive for hope, for along with God's help, they will reach new heights for many years to come.

May 21, 2009

Maxed Out

It's almost become a rare sight anymore that you don't see a youth walking down the street talking into a cell phone. Just the other day, I was sitting on the porch with a neighbor when we noticed a teen skateboarding along the sidewalk chatting with a friend on his cell. So, owning a cell phone is very much a part of our times.

What blew my mind recently are advertisements persuading youngsters to own credit cards. Whoa there, mama! Is this on the up and up?

I contacted two credit card companies, and sure enough, there is no age minimum as to how old one has to be to have this plastic money assigned to him, as long as the card is issued through, and at the parents' discretion.

Not being a member of the modern generation, I have a little trouble allowing children to spend freely using this form of currency, so to speak.

First of all, what ever happened to working and getting an allowance on a weekly basis? I don't feel I had a deprived childhood. I worked hard for my money (sounds like a song title) and was satisfied with my five bucks per week. I saved every dollar I made and spent it wisely on something for which I saved. That money meant something to me and I knew if I set a goal to get merchandise, I would have to do a little planning or I would have to settle for something of lesser quality.

If my parents would have handed me a credit card and told me to spend as I saw fit, I not only would have been shocked, but more carefree, knowing not only were they footing the bill, but I would not have to labor for a few measly bucks.

It goes without saying that the credit card companies promote usage of cards for every member of the family, but is it really healthy? I think not.

Let me illustrate a point by relating a little story about Alice and Ed Eager. It can easily be said that if this couple were to have nicknames, they would be called "Mr. and Mrs. Plastic." Every time they showed up at a restaurant or department store they would purchase something using one of many credit cards. Visiting their home, there were many items purchased years ago for which they had not paid. They had maxed out two or three of their cards on a monthly basis. It was their lifestyle and they had no regrets.

When Billy Eager became six, his parents signed him up for a Capital One card. He was given permission to buy whatever he chose. By the end of the month, he had maxed out his card, but saw nothing wrong with it because mom and dad did it all the time.

What kind of example are parents setting for their children if they permit spending habits to be free-for-alls?

I know of one individual who has to go to therapy on a regular basis because she constantly maxes out her cards, yet, buys and buys and buys using plastic because she is what I call "thing happy." Can you imagine a youth in his early teens having to do the same thing?

"Carding" as I also call it can lead to an addiction. It is so easy to walk up to a counter, plop down the merchandise on a counter, hand over a card, sign the register paper, and then walk out of the door with the items. People do it all the time. It isn't something one can stop at the drop of a hat. But just think if kids are allowed to get swallowed up in this spending habit, where would it eventually lead?

Personally speaking, I think it is wrong to give a child a credit card under ordinary circumstances. One representative from Discover told me she thought it was a good idea, in as much as when youth are on vacation or in a hospital, they can readily get what they need without bothering the parents.

I don't agree. Give the child a certain amount of money and tell him that is all he can spend on the boardwalk, for example. Maybe that value system will click into place. Why would a kid need a credit card in a hospital? Beats me.

Bottom line—teach your kid the value of a buck. The lesson will be invaluable.

October 5, 2006

On Expectation . . .

Thanks!

Today, I'm going to talk about one of my favorite subjects—expectation, and relate how I believe it ties into gift giving.

I think it is indeed rare to find someone on this earth who doesn't expect something from another. When you think about it, our ways of thinking have been patterned by what others do in our society. Whatever we say, do or act will often trigger a response from another in ways we sometimes "expect," and other times in ways we find a little shocking, if not down-right uncalled for and just plain rude.

Let's just take the first option in my survey—"I want to get something in return." Defining the word, "something," may be different to each individual. The recipient may want a hug, a gift, or just a thank you. Maybe the latter should be automatic when a hug or a present is exchanged.

But let's say you've taken great joy into purchasing something for another, and even had a company mail it to the respective party as a surprise, with the words "Merry Christmas," and had the sender disclose your name. But you never heard a peep from the recipient(s). What emotions should go through your mind? Should you erase those feelings of joy? Should you tell another, "That Felix really has a nerve not thanking me for the Christmas present I bought and shipped to him to make sure he got it in time?" Should you let bitterness replace the "giving" spirit?

It happens all the time, doesn't it? Our human nature dictates that we must conduct ourselves according to conditions.

"Of course you must say 'Thanks!'" when someone goes to the trouble of buying or giving a gift to another. "That's only common sense," you may say. But not everyone thinks that way anymore. Now, you may find that appalling, but people are becoming more lax with the formalities of the past.

But, in thinking about it over the years, I have drawn my own conclusions that I think may surprise you.

Marty, wanting to show his appreciation to administrative members of his church, sends each of them some kind of Christmas gift. A matter of fact, making sure it gets there on time, he hand delivers the items to the church office. The gifts are received by the receptionist. Of the four employees, he gets a "thank you" from two.

Here is where it gets contentious. Did any one of the four *ask* Marty to give them gifts? No. It was purely spontaneous on his part. It was a heart-felt act. Since they didn't ask for the gifts, *must* they show their gratitude? Not at all. To give with the expectation of getting something in return, if it's only a thank you, I believe, is having one's heart in the wrong place. You may say, "That's the right thing to do." That is how society has raised us up to believe we should respond to such stimuli. Now, if you have taken the initiative to approach Marty and ask him, "May I have a gift?" and he reciprocates, then there's no question, a "thank you" is definitely in order. But to get something you didn't ask for puts things in a whole different light.

With that being said, should I promote the idea that one stray away from society's norm and cling to my philosophy? Here again, not at all. What I'm trying to do is emphasize that with every coin there is a face value, and a flip side, acts that may occur that will always be contrary to expectation. This is very important. Never set yourself up to believe that your thoughts are going to equal someone else's. Don't position yourself as a conditional giver, and third, and whatever you do, never let go of that joy that exists within you when buying, wrapping and presenting your gift. Maintaining a happy heart will eventually render a happy soul.

May 7, 2009

CORNFLAKES?

As I sat sipping on my coffee one morning, I began to ponder over some of the incidents in my life that resulted in an entirely different twist than I expected.

Way back in junior high school, my brother Bob and I wanted to surprise my mother with something we made in the oven. We decided on brownies. So we dug up the recipe and began reading. Surprisingly, everything that it called for was available in our kitchen. We had it made, so to speak.

So, we went about our mission. Sorting through one ingredient and then another, we carefully followed the instructions. After mixing the works in a bowl, we put them into a pan and proceeded to bake. After the completed time had arrived, we removed the container and put it onto a rack for cooling. All was working out according to our plan.

When my mother arrived home after shopping, we offered her the little square-cut cakes. Very surprised, she hastened over to the counter, grasped one between her fingers, and put it in her mouth. Her expression was priceless. When she quickly took it back out, I asked, "Don't you like it?" With that she exclaimed, "It's not sweet, it's really salty!" Then I realized what I had done. Instead of dumping in the required amount of sugar, I got the containers mixed up and used salt. What a revolting development that turned out to be.

That was just one instance where we expected something good for mom, but it didn't turn out the way we had hoped. But talk about a situation going "topsy-turvy," the following story definitely left an impression in my mind.

Years back, I remember hearing on the news that a man took the life of his wife because she had relocated some food items in the refrigerator without his knowledge. I thought that was a little drastic, to say the least.

But we are a people of habit, there's no doubt about it. That's why people sit in the same seats in church, take walks during a certain time each day, and even eat their meals at certain times.

So, somewhere in my brain cells, that story stuck concerning the man and his dead wife. Now, I want to make it perfectly clear. I love my wife dearly, and would never think of going to any type of drastic measure to even so much as raise my voice if she moved things about in our kitchen. However, with that said, it has happened twice, and it's just a matter of restructuring the mind to think another way, that's all.

One day, it went like this. I was looking forward to my favorite meal—breakfast. I reached into the cupboard for the cereal dishes and felt bigger bowls. Normally, all I have to do is open one of the doors, stick my arm in, and grasp a dish. From there on, I'd have it made. But it certainly didn't work out that way. She had moved these dishes to the next shelf above. To this day, I still have trouble getting used to the new location.

Oh, but it didn't stop there. I like teaspoons and small forks. Opening the drawer and reaching in "where they normally were" was an easy task for me. When my dearest did some reorganization, I cringed, but got used to it. It was far better to adapt than complain.

Word to the wise—Talk it over first?

My third example of many takes me back to my Ashland College (now University) years. At that time, I resided with my parents in Oklahoma. It was Thanksgiving weekend. I couldn't fly home from Ohio since I would need to be back right after the holiday, so I needed someplace to stay since the institution was closed down. Everyone else had gone home.

The college cook so graciously invited me to stay at her house since she had a spare bedroom. I appreciated her gesture and accepted her offer. Actually, I thought I had it made—an experienced cook who knew how to make virtually anything in the kitchen.

On the day of Thanksgiving, I tidied up and sat in my room until she called me down for the feast. Actually, I was famished and couldn't wait. All of a sudden I heard her call my name, "Paul, we're leaving now. See you later." What, no dinner from the friendly, fabulous cook of AC? When I did descend to the kitchen, I rooted through the cupboard to find something to eat. I spent the day watching football and eating Cornflakes.

Be prepared. You, too, will find that things don't always turn out as you may think!

June 22, 2010

STILL SEE YOU!

Now that we are a little over a week away from Christmas, I have been getting overwhelmed by companies sending me catalogs wanting me to purchase items for my *loved ones.*

The one *fad* that seems to be catching on is camouflaging everything. At one time only soldiers and hunters wore this type of clothing so they couldn't be seen by the enemy or animals. But now, the design is everywhere.

One type of apparel that is in demand is camouflage clothing, also known as camo, designed for all aged groups. Toddlers can now wear clothes such as burp bibs, floppy and thermal hats. Gee, is dad taking them hunting, or do they just want to look like their dad?

Just the other day, I noticed the design on long underwear. What is the deal there? If it's not going to be shown as outerwear, what purpose does it have? Wonderful. You have a tree design against your posterior. Not even a spider will be inclined to walk up the trunk of the tree since the clothing will, in most cases, be tucked in one's boot.

I had to laugh when I saw a camo blanket on someone's twin bed. Guess what? It did little to hide the person sleeping in the bed. "I can still see you!"

And why would the material cover a crib? Of all places, I would want to see my baby's actions without his disappearing act under this brown patterned cloth.

Now thermos bottles are made in various shades with camo designs. Great. I'm in the woods, decide to rest, take it out of my knapsack, pour a drink of good, hot vegetable broth and then set it down beside me. I walk ahead to sit on a log to re-strap my boots. After doing that, I turn around to retrieve my bottle, and guess what? I can't find it because it looks like the leaves in which I laid it. Swell.

Walkie-talkies and flashlights have the same problems as the thermoses. Lay them down on the forest floor and they may go unnoticed especially as the sun goes down.

Hey, attention all ATV owners. There are wonderful camouflage designed covers for your vehicles. Just think, you can cover your vehicle while parked in the great outdoors. Just remember where you put it, because if you don't, you may be losing time looking for your mode of transportation.

I noticed they now make camo dog vests. Thank goodness, it doesn't extend over the whole dog, just the mid section. God knew what He was doing when He didn't make fir colored dogs. Someone may think they are moving bushes. I can see an orange vest on a pet, but camo? I don't think that will keep someone from shooting it, in my opinion,

I really can't see the advantage of having seat covers done in camo. The promotional literature may say that the "Water-resistant urethane-coated nylon will keep your seat clear of mud, water and other messes," but so does black, red, brown or gray. It serves no purpose to be camo, as far as I can see.

I guess if one would put the covers on the seats, then he must also put it on his steering wheel. Somehow, that would only make sense to me.

And we can't forget the infant car seat cover. Oh no, infants can't be seen if they are riding in the back seat of their parent's cars. They must be hidden at all times with only their heads peaking from beneath the covers. I guess the animals walking by the vehicles won't suspect there is a child aboard, do you reckon?

We've come a long way since our military introduced the clothing to the public. I can only wonder if my wife will be getting me a camo-colored fishing lure for Christmas!

December 13, 2007

WHAT ARE THE CHANCES?

One of the area's physicians came into my store recently to have a passport photo taken. Upon entering, he received a call on his cell phone and quickly stepped to the next room. I tried to ignore what he was saying, but did hear him expressing his apologies profusely over and over again. When he returned to the studio, he immediately explained what had happened.

He and a number of other doctors were at a luncheon. When the meal was over, my client got up and exited the dining hall. Walking over to the coat rack, he saw what he thought was his garment, took it off the hanger, put it on and departed. Reaching into the pocket of his pants, he pulled out his keys, got into his car and headed toward his office. Somewhere along his journey, he dug in the coat pocket and pulled out a set of car keys. He then realized his mistake and had taken somebody else's coat.

The other physician quickly realized he was in a fix when he could not only locate his coat, but not get into his car as well. He frantically started making some phone calls and was blessed to find that my client had his keys. Talk about embarrassment.

But this wasn't the only time my client had a run-in with bizarre circumstances. He related to me that he and his wife had gone out to eat and asked a valet to park his car at the restaurant. The keys were handed to this employee and the couple entered the door and disappeared.

When they finished eating, they exited and asked for their car and provided a detailed description of it. After seeing what they thought was their car, the couple got in. The gentleman started the motor and they headed toward home. Everything was exactly as they left it, so they thought. Then the Mrs. wanted to read something and the doctor told her that there was a flashlight in the glove compartment. Upon opening it, not only did they not find the flashlight, but also discovered the car was not theirs. Turning around, they took it back immediately and exchanged it for their car. The owner never got wind of the situation, so I was told.

When it comes to picking up the wrong coat, I have to believe this is a common mistake.

After dining with my family in an area restaurant, we hastened to the coat rack, took our coats and headed toward the parking lot. It wasn't two minutes later that my mother-in-law asked me what I had on my coat. Without looking, I told her "I don't have anything on my coat." Then I looked down and saw a sticker from Idlewild Park. This garment that looked just like mine wasn't. Here, too, I raced back, made the exchange and returned to our vehicle. The person still eating had no idea I had made the mistake.

But, if ever there was a story that took the prize, it has to be the next one.

My brother and I were working in a hotel up in Maine. Often we were given the car keys to go on errands for the owners. Some days we would have to travel as far as 60 miles one way to buy food.

The practicality of having two cars was obvious. If we Volkmanns were filling up grocery buggies a good distance away, then one of the other employees could use the other vehicle for another mission. Sometimes we were given both sets of keys. My brother would drive one place, and I another.

One day, I hopped into the Chevy and by mistake inserted the key to the Buick. It slipped in with ease, and turning it, the car's engine started immediately. Now tell me . . . what are the chances of that ever happening?

I have one last suggestion that both the doctor and I recommend for the future—write your names inside your coats. Then you won't be flustered with embarrassment if someone should happen to call and ask, "Do you have my keys?"

May 19, 2005

On Odds and End

ELBY

When it comes to eulogies, I believe I have only written one as long as I have been writing this column. It was about a friend and close associate who shared the same profession—photography.

Since I always have looked at my writings as contributions to the lighter side of life, I seldom discuss political or heavier type subject material that might tend to depress rather than edify. Today is different.

We lost a close member of our family recently, our little 13 year-old Chihuahua named Elby. He died of congestive heart failure. Anyone who has lost a pet can identify with emotions that weighed heavy on the hearts of caregivers, family, and all who knew him. He wasn't just something we had to feed, take to veterinarians or walk on a leash. He was family.

Both our kids grew up with Mr. Elb, as we sometimes called him. To them, he was more than a playmate, a bedfellow or a sidekick. If you ever wanted to picture love in action, seeing the three of them together is a place to start.

One of Elby's many joys in life was visiting my wife's mother. He would sit nestled by her side as she watched television, talked to visitors or even ate meals. Even when my mother-in-law came to visit at our house, Elby would follow her around everywhere. When she sat down, so did he. You could see it in his eyes. He was proud to have her as a friend.

Even when my wife sat and watched television as was a common practice in our household, "our little boy" as we also nicknamed him, would jump up on the couch and lay across her leg. His desire to be by her side was evident right to the end.

There was something about vacuum cleaners that stirred his adrenaline. When my wife would be cleaning one of the rooms, he would run full speed up to her, turn around, and then head back in my direction and then stop and look up at me with the biggest smile on his face. Once I smiled, he would do it over and over again. That wonderful smile touched my heart in so many ways.

Whenever I announced to Elby the arrival of our children, Kelsey from Baltimore, or Aaron from Pittsburgh, he would stand motionless in the living room looking up at the window, hoping what I was telling him was about to happen. He would then proceed to the top of the staircase and look down 13 steps to the front door. Ever so slowly his tail would begin to wag, anticipating their arrival. After seeing one of them come in the door, he would scurry down as fast as his little legs could carry him with the biggest smile any dog of his size could muster. All the while, he would wag his tail with such speed that one could sense all the excitement within him. He then would jump four or five times straight in the air, over 20 inches at a shot. No one could ever question his thrill.

And if one mentioned one of two words, walk or cage, he would literally spring out of his little circular bed on all fours and head down the steps in anticipation of fulfilling one of his foremost dreams. He loved the great outdoors and often accompanied me on my adventures.

Our backyard was his domain. I don't care if it was a squirrel, rabbit or bird, nothing was allowed to trespass on our property and he made every possible effort to catch the critters, even though he never succeeded. It was laughable, at best, to watch.

Many people would come up to me while we were on our walks and ask, "Can I pet the puppy?"

All were amazed when we told them he was 13 and far from being a youngster.

Elby did have his jealous moments that amused us immensely. When my wife and I would hug, he would protest, jumping straight up and barking as he did so. Was he trying to tell us he disapproved of our closeness? That certainly seemed to be the case.

I could probably go on and on and on. Our family had a fantastic relationship with "man's best friend." We will not only miss his love and devotion, but also the many ways he affected our day to day lives. I can only hope that we meet again and he will share that beautiful smile with us.

October 2, 2008

Floored the Pedal

No sooner had I hopped onto my three-wheeled vehicle than I was making my way down one of the aisles of a well-known area store. This mode of transportation was different for me. All other times, one would find me pushing a grocery cart or grasping a number of items until my hands could hold no more.

As my son walked beside me, I found it difficult to catch up to him. He also seemed to be somewhere off in the distance. But as usual, he would stop, wait, and then repeat his escape once again.

Not only was I finding shopping a little more challenging, considering I was sitting rather than standing, but I was seeing items from a whole different perspective. On top of that, I was operating a battery-powered piece of equipment. I had all but given up on the idea that shopping would be so easy and all I had to do was to sit on this motorized device and push a button that would then thrust me forward. Life cannot be defined as being in the fast lane, as the saying goes. With that mechanism, the maximum speed may reach one mile per hour, if that. But I was moving forward or backward and I didn't have to tire my muscles in search of food, light bulbs or anything else the store may offer.

One thing that caught me off guard was going in reverse. Not only could I virtually travel at the same speed, but I had a little added treat. As I thumbed the reverse button, a beeping noise accompanied my action. All of a sudden, I felt I was standing beside a backhoe or a cement truck backing in reverse. A sense of power came over me. "Hey there people. Watch out. The Peev is doing his thing. Stand aside."

Maybe I should have traveled backwards throughout the store. Wherever I would go, people, I'm sure, would be wondering, "What is that beeping sound we keep hearing throughout the store?" I think my neck would get sore after awhile if I were always looking behind me. And Lord forbid, what would happen if I toppled a banana rack while looking one way and not seeing such a display on my blind side? And if I kept looking behind me, people could easily steal my goods out of my basket without me ever knowing it. Wonder if I had a purse? Snatchers would have a field day with me. What would I tell the cops upon their arrival? "Well, it was like this officer. I floored the pedal and was racing down the aisle of this market, going one quarter to one half of a mile per hour backwards when all of a sudden I turned around and my purse was gone. Lord have mercy. Who could have been so bold in midday as to steal my handbag without me ever knowing? It sure beats me."

"Backwards?" the sergeant blurted out.

I was hoping he hadn't caught that nine-letter word.

Blushing a bit, I had to confess the truth. I know someone would eventually catch me in a lie, so I thought it best to be up front.

All of a sudden, I felt guilty.

"Yes sir," looking smack dab right into his eyes. Maybe being polite would be a virtue here. I heard it was always good to show respect and be honest. If ever there was a place to be so, this definitely was the place.

"Why in God's name would you ever want to drive full throttle backwards down the aisles of a store such as this?" he asked me.

I didn't mean to be smart with him, but I again tried to be polite stating, "Could you please leave God out of the picture in this case. I didn't do this in God's name. I did so because I felt powerful driving a vehicle that moved me with no effort. All I had to do was sit, work two thumbs, watch and listen. Hearing the reverse tones when I backed up was an extra added plus."

"But shouldn't you be acting your age?" he suggested.

I guess I never thought of that in my moment of bliss, if I wished to call it that.

The way I see it, sometimes it's good to do things out of character as long as no harm is done, right?

March 1, 2007

Parting Can't Be Easy . . .

Anytime two people part in a relationship, it can't be easy. It's been about two months now that Ken and Barbie have gone their own ways. Just to imagine how each must feel after such pampering must be devastating to both of them.

Here was Barbie. She was well dressed, cuddled, fed, and cared for all her life. She had no burdens in the world. Every little girl in our country was making sure the slender-legged beauty was pampered beyond anyone's expectations.

If anyone would look at the wardrobe of this playmate, it was quick to be known that this blond doll had more clothes than most teenagers did growing up. Each youngster probably changed the clothes on this young lady four or five times a day. What a life!

And what about Ken, Barbie's soul mate? Who would have ever thought that after 40 some years, the two of them would drift apart? Both were fixtures in our childhood. As one of the stanzas of Frank Sinatra's song went, "You can't have one without the other."

Now, I'm beginning to wonder if either of them can actually dress themselves. After all, for two decades, both were dressed and undressed several times a day. I have a feeling that this famous couple never left sight of the other. Digging into the depths of my gray matter, I even have glimpses of children making Ken kiss Barbie or vice-versa. Surely, they must have given each other hugs (with the help of their owners, of course).

On the agony of separation . . . There wasn't even a trial run to see if the two could live apart for a short amount of time. No . . . the promoters had to be playing the cold turkey trick on this famous pair. One has to feel sorry for one or both of them. How could each be holding up now without the other's companionship?

According to my perception, a typical day's conversation may have gone as such:

"Morning, Barbie," Ken's voice echoed across the room. "Hi there, Ken," Barbie called over to him. "Isn't it great God has given us a new day to share our lives together? Say, have you seen Randy and Lucy yet? They usually come in to see if we are awake and need anything."

It wouldn't be long thereafter that the kids would wake up and spend some of their day's attention delighting in clothing the renowned couple any way they saw fit.

But now things are quite different. Where do you suppose Ken is hanging out? Does Barbie have to stay dressed in her same attire or is there someone still caring for her needs? Do the two ever get to see each other? I wonder if they call each other on the phone? If so, would Barbie be talking to Ken as soul mates talk or would she stay cool? "Hey there, honey-bunny," she would proclaim. "Are you still that handsome hunk?" I know it wouldn't be that, "Hello, Ken, how are you? I am fine" routine. These two were the ultimate. There was no separation between them. Where you found one, you found the other. Now all I imagine are screams in the night from both of them. "Ken, where are you? Are you all right? I miss you . . ." "Barbie," "Wherever you are, I pray you are being taken care of in every sense of the word, and you are all right. I wish you were with me again."

And so it goes . . . there is nothing easy about parting, particularly when two beings (if you want to call Ken and Barbie that) are forced to separate beyond one's control. The only thing left to do is to make the best of the situation and look forward. I'm sure this couple could write books concerning all their memories. But now, new chapters have begun. Maybe they'll create something special with each new relationship.

February 23, 2004

Mr. T. Gets Hung

Recently, I was given the task of framing a piece of the turf that came from Three Rivers Stadium in Pittsburgh.

Affixed to it were photographs of memorabilia plus tickets and a tie pin from the 1976 football season.

As I looked down at this 14-inch square material, I started to imagine just what happened on this turf 30 years ago.

Then I began to personalize it a little more. I thought of it more than something to be stepped on. This was a piece of history that if it could talk, could certainly reveal nightly activities before and after the games, weekend activities and noises of shouting and cheering some of which would be printable and some not.

Imagine "Turf's" (also known as Mr. T.) total experience with his first introduction to the architectural masterpiece and the many years to follow. Little did he realize as being sewn together that he would be in the limelight of activities and play such an important role.

I'm sure when Mr. T. originally entered the picture, he (or she) never would have thought that so much would have gone on in the center of those concrete walls. I sense that he would do his thing, lay around, occasionally have a visitor, get a good cleaning once in awhile, watch the light of the sun come up in the east and settle in the west.

When Turf was called to duty one fair afternoon, he knew what was ahead of him. Like all other artificial ground, he realized that it was man for him to join a union. All these guys had to stick together. If one fell out of line, something was done about it right away. Mr. T. recognized that fact, and as a result, maintained his best behavior.

But how easy can that be? When sports teams work out, slide and bounce on him, it must leave a real impact. In addition, when rock bands come in and youth tramp all over him (I keep calling him that gender because that's the way writing is—I don't want feminists to get mad at me), it can't be easy.

Visualize a big stage set up on top of Turf with lots of equipment, lights and a constant jumping on the platforms. That certainly can't be an easy thing to take.

On the other hand, think of the other goings-on that fill the air as spectators flock to the Northside where they are assured of a seat even though some may find themselves looking down from "Peanut Heaven."

But one thing was for sure. They always got a glimpse of Mr. T.

Turf's "lay and waiting" game didn't always bring pleasant memories. There were times he was stomped on repeatedly by girls jumping on him to see their favorite rock stars, ball players pouncing on him to make a spectacular catch or slide after the reception was made. Then came the "not so pretty" events when athletes actually bloodied a knee or even a nose in his fibers, leaving a reddening color in his untarnished appearance.

Sometimes, he could see it coming. What would you do if you knew some guy was about to land on top of you face-first, or dig his elbow into your core in a second's flash? Probably the same thing Turf did, lay there and take it. What else can one do?

But like all things, nothing lasts forever. With the upcoming news of the implosion of his once founded home, the union was dissolved, and his fellow mates were lifted from where they were laid to rest. In a sense, it was a sad time, because being a member of the team became a lifestyle. There were always things to which to look back; lots of entertainment, festivals of all kinds and even a bit of attention given to Turf on occasion. He liked that. He was proud of the fact that he had seniority, holding his ground through thick and thin. There is something to be said for that.

And now, as Mr. T. hangs somewhere on the wall in a wood and glass enclosure, he may not sense the patterns of nature, nor hear the crowd noises or feel the pounding feet of high school and professional ball players. But, I'll bet he'll never forget hearing the cheers for Roberto Clemente, the Steel Curtain, Franco Harris' Immaculate Reception, L.C. Greenwood and many other famous musicians who brought enthusiasm to the Stadium.

Yes, Mr. Turf, you did your job and you did it well. May those who view you now do so with pride. I have to say, you deserve it!

March 3, 2001

THIS IS THE CITY

The story you are about to read is true.

This is the city, Latrobe, Pennsylvania. I work here. I carry a notebook.

It was Friday, March 17th. It was a cold day in Latrobe. We were working the night shift in District Four.

The boss's name was Chief Charles Huska. The officer with whom I rode was Patrolman Bernie Froio. My name is Volkmann.

The officer was doing an excellent job patrolling the streets and alleys of Latrobe. I was trying to do my thing as well to the best of my ability, write a story as to how our city is protected by our well-trained work force.

But police work wasn't entirely new to me. Back in the late 60's, I attended Police Officers' Training School and became certified in law enforcement in the state of Ohio.

So, I was curious to note the differences of riding in a cruiser now, as compared to then.

Chief Huska informed me about the City's Ride Along Program, and I immediately took him up on it.

That designated evening, I met Officer Froio in front of the Latrobe Police Department and we proceeded to tour his assigned area. It didn't take long to realize that the cars in which I used to patrol, are a far cry from today's vehicles.

Our "black and whites" were limited to a car radio, shotgun, a notebook compartment and a few miscellaneous items in the trunk.

Here was evidence of living in a "high-tech" world. Equipped within this unit was an intricate system of communication enabling police to gather and relate information quickly.

Behind me was a plastic barrier dividing the officer from passengers in the back. This is called the safety cage. Froio emphasized, "You need it," he said. "People nowadays from kids to seniors have no respect. If we didn't have the shield, we could be attacked or even spit on," he pointed out.

The Shippensburg University graduate explained other major differences in his and my training.

Police officers now have to complete 640 hours of training. I only had to do 144. A college degree is now mandatory. "Today when one week is spent in class, the next is on the rifle range," he said. Ours was 90 percent class work. Today's officers have to be experts with shotguns, revolvers, and automatic weapons; we only had to score well with revolvers." And the list goes on . . .

I was highly impressed with my chauffeur in detailing departmental procedures, explaining job responsibilities and handling incidents.

As I ended my tour, Froio extended an invitation to others. "I encourage other citizens of Latrobe to ride along so people REALLY get to see what we do," he pointed out.

So there we have it, the facts. I wanted only the facts, and I got them!

March 25, 2000

(This was my first published story for the Latrobe Bulletin)